Fist Of Destiny - Memoirs of

**by
Karl Lancaster**

**Published by
Lancaster Publishing**

through Createspace

Copyright 2013

Dedication

I have so many people who I should dedicate this book to but if I did the dedication would be book length as well! So I will try and keep it to the few people who made a big impression on me one way or another but will break it up between four categories :-

Family - my father John, who I never had enough time with, my mother Elsie who was always there for me and my wife Trisha and our sons Joshua and Luke. Also the whole of the Sweetman family and it's offshoots and my stepfather Bob.

Friends - Steve Burr for the endless what if's, Stuart for the drinks and George for introducing me to the gym. Kay for being a friend for so long.

Martial art friends and colleagues - Noel Reece for being my friend and pupil, Dave Miller, Susan Miller, Phil and Jim Newcombe for great times. Colin Dunn (ex European champ) for being my friend and a dam good kick boxer, Bob Allen (ex world champion) for being a pain in the arse. Ed, Gary, Kevin, Adam, Ting, Andy Lee, Andy Denney, Shu and Errol for being my brothers and sisters and for all your help and support.

Martial Instructors - Sifu Lu Jun Hai for being the ultimate inspiration and teacher, Irvin Cleydon for cultivating a very silly young boy and for being my life long friend and Terry Parker for being a great instructor and good guy.

In Memory of

John France, instructor and friend and gone too soon

Brian Devlin, instructor and hard man

Harry, friend and fellow pupil of Sifu Lu

Foreword

Looking back, my earliest childhood memory is one of me riding a three wheeled bike down Church Street Market, Marylebone, just off the Edgware Road. A shame really, because I mentioned it to my mum once, and she was adamant that it never happened. So, like a lot of things its almost certainly a fiction, something I dreamed up and convinced myself was real. A lot of people do that, and martial artists are no exception.

What I want to do here in these writing's is to give a nuts and bolts view of a martial artists life. What drove me to do martial arts, who I idolized, what I liked, hated, what made me sad. And along the way I want to blow away a few myth's. I also hope to inspire others to try the martial arts, or to succeed at them, or even just to view their own chosen sport, or even just their life, in a different way.

Also, as I spin out my own story, I would like to enlighten the reader where I can. This may seem a little presumptuous for some, but my aim is not to 'teach my granny to suck eggs', but to enrich the basic martial artist and non martial artist's alike. I hope to do this partly with my own experience, partly by rehashing the history, philosophy and application of those arts I have been directly involved with.

I also want to recount some stories about martial artists I have known or who have had influence on me, be it all through a third or even 'forth' party. During the telling of this narrative I want to tell of some of the remarkable things instructors and great masters have done. But I also want to dispel some of the rubbish which has been put about. This last part may upset some people, and I will apologize now if I offend, it's not my aim, but it may be my duty to do so at times.

Karl Lancaster March 2009

Chapter One - The Big Boss

I was born (no surprise there then) on 13th November 1955 and, after some argument, named Karl Lancaster. My father wanted me to be called Charles, but my mother had other ideas, so they settled on Karl which is the Germanic equivalent anyway. Things did not go right from the off as my name was to be spelled with a 'c', the Scandinavian spelling, but the registrar mucked it up.

My father was John Patrick Lancaster. He hated the Patrick bit, his mother had been born in Ireland near Cork, but as he hated the Irish he would never accept that she was truly a Celt. If you ever wanted to cause an argument you had only to bring up his Celtic ancestry and he was off! As the name Lancaster implies the family was English and probably originally from Lancashire, although no one could remember back that far.

Apparently, according to my father, the more recent ancestors of the Lancaster family had been Fishermen and it was a family tradition to take a Scandinavian bride. However, as I allude to in my foreword, we often make assumption or even down right fiction fact. And I could find no record of fisherman or Danish brides when researching my family tree. Only that my great great grandfather (I think) was described as a 'gentleman', which, in those days was rare.

According to my father, my great grandmother spoke with an obvious Danish accent her whole life. And it was no doubt the Scandinavian blood (if it existed) that contributed to my fathers looks. On holiday he was always mistaken for German, a fact that peed him off his entire life.

My grandfather Richard was born in Woolwich London in 1905. Hence the now family tradition of being an Arsenal supporter. Granddad Richard also decided to become a police officer. At six feet two inches and probably about 15 or 16 stone he was a big guy (although the smallest of all his brothers) and ideally suited to being an old time copper. He was by all accounts a total bastard and not someone to mess with. Apparently one of his past times was to start a fight in a pub, let it escalate in to a small riot and then call in the cavalry and nick the lot of them. He also used to carry a pistol. Its from Granddads time at least that the family have a tradition of fighting and of being handy with a gun. Unfortunately I never met my grandfather or grandmother, or indeed step grandmother as they all died by fifty. My grandfather dying the year I was born.

My father was one of three, the other two being girls. Like his father he grew up to be a powerfully build man and stood well over six feet tall. He didn't have such a good start in life, his mother died when he was young and his dad remarried. Apparently his step mum was quite well to do and he loved her but she also died young.

Dad was not a well child. He spent several years in

hospital with childhood asthma. But at fourteen he became the second youngest recruit to join the Royal Navy. He spent ten years in the Navy, mostly as a submariner. During that time he boxed for the navy, shot for the navy (he was a marksman with at least three confirmed kills) and played water polo for the navy. He also learned unarmed combat and more importantly, how to fight.

One thing my dad wasn't shy of was a fight. All through his life he was happy to accommodate. Even at nearly fifty he was able to knock a guy down with one punch.

In contrast to my dad who was big, blonde and blue eyed, my mother was short, dark and brown eyed. She was also shrewd, hard working and had a very bad temper! She once chased one of her sister around with a red hot poker. And on another occasion I watched her bury a fork in my fathers hand. They got on like 'Ali' and 'Fraser' and some of the fights were just as good but did nothing for me as an only child in a constantly warring family.

If my father's heritage was colourful it paled in contrast to my mothers family. Latin, Celtic, French and Jewish were the predominant contributors to the blood line.

My maternal great-grandfather fought in the first world war as part of a cavalry unit. He was shot and gassed and eventually died of his wounds. My great-grandmother also died young. But that was my mothers family. My mothers fathers family boasted an endearing great grandfather who was virtually illiterate who was dominated by a self centered would be actress wife. Both lived well in to their eighties.

Both my mothers parents had a great influence on my life as I virtually lived with them until I was about eleven years old. My grandfather was domineering and quick tempered, but a typical bully who backed down when a more able man was about, funny but he never got on with my father. He was far more fond of animals than he was people and bred dogs, birds and fish. He was also a very selfish man. But he did have good points like taking me for long walks to museums and parks on a Saturday morning when my dad was working or in the pub, and my mum was out with her sisters and my grandmother down Oxford Street. The other good point was he enjoyed wrestling and every Saturday afternoon we would sit there and watch the likes of Kendo Nagasaki and Big Daddy pretend to hurt each other. Although totally bogus, but a lot more technical than the modern day American wrestling, it did give me some insight in to 'fighting systems' at an early age.

I'm sure it was due to my childish interest in wrestling that my father one day decided to teach me boxing. In his eyes boxing was the combat art for a man, although he was vaguely aware of more complete systems of combat like judo and karate, but had no direct dealings with them other than through the minimal unarmed combat training he got in the Navy.

My boxing training started when I was about 14 years old and mainly consisted of my dad giving me tips on strength exercises, shadow boxing and sparring, during which he would thump hell out of one of my arms. To be fair we never used gloves and he was being pretty gentle, it just didn't feel like that at the time.

Unlike some of the kids today, by 14 I had already had my fair share of fights. At primary school I had both given and received a few good beatings. And out of school I was not the most popular kid on the block and this too resulted in a few good tear ups!

Things didn't change when I moved from Christ Church Primary to Rutherford Comprehensive. Rutherford had a reputation even then, and it endures now. I was never one of the big fighters at school, I was too shy and somewhat slight. But I did surprise a few people with my punch and stopped several playground opponents with just the one shot.

In about 1972/73 I got my first look at the new must see cinema craze, oriental martial arts film. If I remember rightly the first film I saw was 'The One Arm Swordsman'. The second was 'Fist of Fury' with the now legendary Bruce Lee. I'm sure by the time I saw it he had already come to an untimely end.

Of course I loved it, like any kid would. And my best friend Tony Christopher and I would spar and make up our own 'kung fu' moves. I was somewhat surprised that although he was bigger than me and a better playground fighter, I could hold my own against him and quite often get the better of him with my homemade martial arts.

Its fair to say that Bruce Lee and also David Carradine in 'Kung Fu' were two very big factors in my life at that time. I went for the whole martial arts things hook, line and sinker! I was so keen my mother brought me home a book on karate. And my father taught me the few bits of unarmed combat he knew.

At that time I knew only what I saw in kung fu films and in the TV series. Of course both, although having a basic element of the philosophy and technique, were wildly inaccurate but entertaining! I recently watched 'Fist of Fury' again and was not only appalled by the acting but also by the technique. Even Bruce looked like an amateur. David Carradine at the time 'Kung Fu' was made didn't know any martial arts at all, although he has learned kung fu since.

But at that time I wasn't aware that David Carradine was a dancer choreographed by another, or that Bruce was more or less self taught with a minimum of actual kung fu training. All I saw was guys who could beat the shit out of other people and appear not only tranquil but also fully justified at the end of it.

Of course the fact they had good bodies and health was also another reason to idolise them. And being famous for kicking arse was yet another pull! Being hailed the best fighter in the world was bound to catch my interest too, even if Bruce wasn't. But alas, I couldn't find a nearby club.

Never one to give up I kept looking for kung fu clubs and lo and behold there was one just a ten minute walk away. But it wasn't cheap. At eighteen I left school and got a job as a clerk with the National Coal Board, working out of their HQ behind Buckingham Palace. I was on a reasonable wage for my age and upper most in my mind was using some of that money to join the kung fu club. But as luck would have it my martial arts career was about to take a totally different route!

I had only been working for the NCB for a month or two when I noticed one of the guys in my building had put up a notice about starting a martial arts club. It was something called aikido and apparently it used the force of the opponent against him. I had never heard of it but thought I would give it a go anyway. And so my kung fu training went on hold for about 25 years!

Chapter Two- The Way of the Harmonious Spirit

On a Thursday night sometime in October 1974 I donned a silly looking white suit, which was too small for me, and stepped on to a martial arts mat for the first time. I had no idea what I was getting myself in to!

Like all aikido sessions we started by bowing to the instructor, who on this occasion was a senior student of the actual instructor. After a brief explanation of what was going to happen we started a series of warm up exercises followed by an introduction to break falls.

One of the guys was a yellow belt and he looked so cool, even though he hadn't done it for long. I later found out his name was David Miller, we have been friends ever since. As it turned out, cool as he was that night, I actually got my first dan black belt about six months before him or in fact before any of the guys who joined around that time.

I met my instructor, Irvine Cleydon the following week. Within two or three weeks I was travelling to other clubs and before the year was out I was training up to five times a week.

At this point I would like to do a little potted history of aikido, and in particular my part in it. For those who know nothing about aikido it has its roots back in 12th century Japan and the rise of the Samurai and their many martial practices.

Daito Ryu Aiki jutsu was apparently founded by a Japanese prince. In reality its probably another case of attributing something to the royal family in order to make it look good and give it some sort of royal seal of approval. Anyway, whatever the origins it did become a well established and practical form of combat which survived through to the 20th century.

Morehei Uyeshiba learned the system, amongst others. And from this developed what came to be known as aikido. Now this is where I may upset a few people, especially aikido practioners.

Its long been held that Uyeshiba, a very good martial artist in his day, studied several Japanese martial systems, including aiki jutsu and used these to develop aikido. Aikido then went through several transformations before he held it up as a complete system. Of course Uyeshiba also claimed he went through a mystical revelation which also changed the emphasis of the art from purely combative to universal love. Here we go then, firstly not all aikidoka subscribe to the universal love bit. And secondly aikido has probably got a lot of Chinese influence in it!

Now I have your full attention, let me explain further. Aikido has several schools it has been split in to. Some of those schools or styles take Uyeshiba's later teachings as their lead. But some of the earlier developed schools like Tomiki and Yoshinkan aikido take the more practical and active combat elements of the art to heart.

Yoshinkan appears on the surface to be quite close to the 'home' style Uyeshiba finalised. That is until you attempt to practice it and find out how much more practical and violent it is. While Tomiki, or sport aikido, and its later branches have a more competitive edge, although in a lot of clubs retaining that combat edge to it as well. It is Tomiki that I was taught.

Most of the people I trained with in Tomiki style, and later in Yoshinkan style, were not your 'peace be on to you' types, all they wanted was an effective fighting system. And this attitude flies in the face of Uyeshiba's later ideas.

For those people with little knowledge of aikido it differs from other Japanese arts in several ways. Its circular, not linear like modern karate. The movements are quite soft and relaxed. And the use of internal force or ki is taught. None of these ideas are common to modern Japanese martial arts.

The probable reason for this was identified by T K Francis, an authority on Chinese internal martial arts, but also a black belt in aikido. As he rightly points out Uyeshiba was a good martial artist and also studied several systems, it seems unlikely that given the chance to expand his knowledge he wouldn't do so. And for several years, while in the army in China he had such an opportunity.

Francis is of the opinion that while serving in China Uyeshiba had the opportunity to see and practice some of the Chinese internal arts, some of the most sophisticated martial systems devised. In all probability it was Bagua that Uyeshiba was exposed to and he incorporated some of the concepts in to aikido. This would fit with the aikido concept of leading ki (or chi) which is fundamental to the system but also at odds to other Japanese systems. The idea of leading chi is probably most familiar to practitioner's of Tai Chi Chuan when incorporated in to the 'pushing hands' exercise.

In practice, and when used as a proper combat system, rather than a vehicle of 'love', aikido is a specialised branch of ju jutsu. It incorporates mainly wrist, elbow and shoulder locks and throws to defeat an opponent. However, there other techniques incorporated including strikes but these are often not seen in the 'softer' versions of the art. Both Yoshikan and Tomiki aikido do retain these harder elements.

Like judo, aikido boasts that it uses the enemy's own power against them selves. Principally this means that if someone wants to push you, you don't resist you go with the direction of the push and the same goes for pull. By speeding up the persons attack and, or, redirecting it you can throw the opponent with ease. Similarly to several Chinese internal styles aikido uses circular movements to avoid, parry and counter an attack. The circles allowing for movement in small areas as well as large and also for the transmission of huge amounts of power.

As well as opened handed techniques, which can be performed standing or kneeling, there are also techniques with and against the knife, bo staff and sword. And many people do not realise that much of the fundamental footwork and movement is based on that used in aiki ken or aikido sword play.

In principle aikido is a stunning martial art, and there have been many displays by top masters which have impressed the martial arts world. But, note I said top masters. It is only Uyeshiba and some of his top pupils that have been able to capture the imagination in this way.

For the average student Aikido is very difficult to learn, let alone master. Even black belts can be little more than mediocre in their application of the art and few can use it in a full on combat situation.

That said I remember my early years in Aikido as being full of pain! My first and principle instructor Irvine Cleydon was very much in the old martial artist tradition. That said he was no street fighter, but nor was he a bully or a pretender. He was just a martial artist who believed in total involvement in his art and the extension of that art in to his daily life.

Irvine was one of two brothers, both gifted in aikido but in totally different ways. I was unlucky in that Peter, Irvine's brother, had left to live in Australia just months before I started. However I did meet him a few years down the line. Peter was the fighter, while Irvine the technician. Peter was a leader to Irvine's politician. Peter was a battering ram to Irvine's rapier. Peter was also the kind of guy that, when surrounded by several muggers, had pissed himself laughing so much at their attempt to intimidate him that they decided they had other things to do and bolted for it.

Of course in those days Peter wasn't the only nutty martial artist about. During the making of the James Bond film You Only Live Twice the film makers had flown over a dozen or so experts in Japanese martial arts. There were connections between our Aikido set up and them and apparently some of the Japanese were taken on a little pub crawl. It didn't start too well when, as they passed a club in Soho, a doorman made a derogatory remark about oriental's and one of them went for him. He dashed back in to the club and slammed a wooden door shut, only to find a fist going right through it. On the same night, when the party split up, one of the Aikido instructors found himself with a Japanese exponent of Karate when they were confronted by a gang of skinheads. The unfortunate leader of the gang found himself on the way to hospital with two broken legs!

In Tomiki there are four distinct phases, movement practice, ki practice, kata and free practice. Peter excelled at free practice, which included various forms of sparring. Irvine on the other hand was just as good at kata, the basic sets of techniques which aikido and many other martial arts use to encapsulate the essence of the system.

Like I said Irvine was totally involved in what he did. And, just like the old masters, his teaching did not stop when the lesson did.

Most people who have never been involved in martial arts have the mistaken idea that it's adherents are pure in mind and body, that their body is a temple and disgusting substances, like alcohol and tobacco would never pass their lips....WRONG! Even the world renowned Shaolin Monks are allowed to drink (although in their case it was by special dispensation from the Chinese Emperor). There is even a fairly well known story about a Chinese kung fu master who was having a couple of drinks with friends while sitting on a windowsill, half way through a conversation the friends looked away from him and when they looked back he wasn't there, it was a one storey fall and they looked out the window expecting to see him dead or injured below. As they did he strolled back in the room totally unharmed. In his intoxicated state he had leaned back, fallen, rolled and climbed back to the room he had fallen from all in a matter of seconds!

Maybe it's just me and I get attracted to the wrong people, but all the martial arts I have done are normally capped off with a visit to the pub. Aikido was no exception. In fact over the years we organised a few pub crawls. It was on one of these we felt Irvine's wrath for letting our guard down.

It was on the surface a pretty silly thing we did. About four or five of us chatted to some Scandinavian tourists who wanted directions, there were a few of them and they surrounded us as we gave them instructions of how to get to their destination. After they had gone Irvine went ballistic, pointing out how we could have been attacked from any direction! He was right of course and I paid more attention to his instructions on and off the mat after that. Even today I normally stay on the outside of a circle of people and I always sit facing the door of a pub or restaurant when ever I can.

Chapter Three - Growing up the Aikido way

I have already mentioned my life long friend Dave Miller in the previous chapter. Dave was from Edinburgh and had only recently moved down to London. His accent wasn't the worse one I had heard but still confused me at times. But he was a nice guy, if a total mess most of the time and a bit of a geek.

To be honest Dave was the first non English person I had really had any great dealings with. Having been brought up in an exclusively white area of London I had not come across many people other than white Londoners.

I can remember when I was about nine or ten years old playing in the playground of my primary school, Christ Church, when the whole of the school was stunned in to silence. We ran to the fence that surrounded the playground to watch one lone Black man walk passed, for most of us it was a first! And even at my secondary school non whites were in a minority and tended to stick together.

So as a Scot Dave stuck out quite a bit, well for me at least. We soon became good friends, and because we were close together age wise (Dave being three or four years older than me) and also in our starting times in aikido, we soon looked for each other on the mat when we needed a partner.

At about the same time we started several other guys started including an even bigger geek than Dave called Neil McDonald. Neil was an odd looking guy with bulging eyes and the weirdest feet I have ever seen. But we hung out together for several years. Two brothers and a couple of friends also started within a few weeks of us starting, the brothers were Phil and Jim Newcombe. They would also feature in my life for the next few years, and Phil and Jim would go on to become high ranking aikidoka and establish them selves as top medallist's at the aikido world championships.

Back in those days life was simple. I spent all day at a job I hated sitting behind a desk trying not to let my brain dissolve. Monday to Friday I spent doing aikido. And at the weekends I went to a pub, a club, or a party, or if it was a good one ….all three!

After a few months of doing aikido under Irvine Cleydon at the National Coal Board club, BBC club and UCL club we added a further club at the civil service facility in Victoria. And then Dave and I pushed the boat out and started to visit another instructor Ahmeed Saeed. Although Ahmed was with the same organisation Irvine was, the Aikido Development Society, they didn't see quite eye to eye for several reasons. Ahmed had committed a great sin by leaving our organisation and training with another rival group, the British Aikido Association, in order to get his black belt. Although no where near as good at, or knowledgeable of kata as

Irvine, Ahmed had trained with the likes of Ken Broom and brushed his randori practice to a high standard. He also trained in a slightly more traditional aikido manner when it came to developing free techniques. And it was because of this that Dave and I decided to train under him.

Ahmed was an Iranian but had an English wife back then and very much English values. He was a big guy, about six feet tall and heavy built and he used his strength when it suited him on the mat, along with a suppleness you didn't expect of someone of his size. And he didn't take prisoners!

Where Irvine would structure the class in a particular way, bringing several elements of aikido in to play on a regular basis, Ahmed was more free flowing and inclined towards free practice and randori. Ahmeed would push us taking us on individually and in pairs and exhausting us to the point we could hardly stand and, in the early days, without allowing us to throw him even once. I can remember distinctly on one occasion being so knackered and frustrated after 20 minutes of trying to throw him that I was nearly in tears but also just intent on knocking his block off before he halted the session. Irvine's lessons were of a shorter duration but just as painful. Several bits of teeth are probably still imbedded in a few tatami mat's because I didn't pick up on what he was trying to teach me quickly enough!

Not long after visiting Ahmeed I also started to train occasionally with another of the association's instructors, John France. John was a real character and fun to be around. But he was also a very strong aikidoka. He was also one of those enquiring minds who was always looking for a better way to perform a move or a train a technique. This quest for something more took John to Shorinji Kempo (the Japanese version of Shaolin kung fu), several styles of aikido, jodo (Japanese stick fighting), iaido (the art of drawing and cutting with the Japanese sword) and kyudo (Japanese archery). I was lucky enough to be instructed by John in both jodo and iaido.

As I said, John was a delight to be around and he was always joking. But a real rough diamond, typical working class with a heart of gold.

So, there I was running around like a blue arsed fly five days a week, seeing as many as three different instructors and still managing to fit the pub and clubs in now and then. Well a bit more than now and then!

To illustrate a point let me taken you through a typical week in my first year or so of aikido. Sunday, first day of the week and, whoopee, no training. So, a nice lay in until about 10 am. Get up, bit of cereal, and about 1145 am a ten minute stroll with my dad, down to The Beehive pub in Homer Street. Five minutes of waiting for it to open, at which point normally joined by old school friend Dave Murphy and several other regulars. In to the pub where my beer was almost certainly already waiting in my own pewter mug. I would then beat Dave at darts before heading over to join my dad and cribbage partner at the card table. About three or four pints later we would head home for Sunday lunch, complete with a glass or two of wine.

Sunday afternoon would crawl by until about 645pm at which point I would head back to the pub, probably to meet Dave again and shortly be joined by my date who would have, at last, come out of an afternoon nap. More darts, crib or dominoes and another four or five pints and home again.

Monday…yuk…work. More soul destroying crap. But lightened a little by going to the canteen and then the bar with Neil McDonald and sometimes joined by Phil Newcombe, couple of quick pints and back to the grind. Then in the evening straight on to the Civil Service club for aikido and a few pints in the club bar after.

Tuesday work, bar, work, aikido, pub. Wednesday, work, bar, work, aikido, pub. Thursday, yep you got it, same again. Friday, surprise same again. Saturday….oops nearly kept going, but no aikido that day nor work!

Saturday was an interesting day. Up about 9am and then helped my dad prepare Saturday's evening meal. After that we went to the pub, four or five pints. Home. Dinner, a stew, homemade meat pie or something like that.

Now, there are from here several possibilities. All of which could be interesting. So you will have to bear with me on this while I run through each one.

Possibility number one - pub (bet you didn't see that coming). The Beehive on a Saturday night could be very entertaining! It was only a small pub, 30 people and it was pretty full! The manager, Gordon, thought he was a hard nut, but far from it, but a nice enough guy, although a little caustic. He did have a very large redeeming feature, his wife Jan. Jan she was gorgeous!

The Beehive was one of those melting pots of society. On any night you could walk in there and find people from 18 to 80 and from every background and career. Dustmen, solicitors, accountants, lorry drivers, shop workers, gangsters, ex boxers, businessmen, bankers, policemen, builders etc, etc, etc. All of them chatting, playing darts, playing cards, drinking together and occasionally fighting together.

I could write a book on the characters in that pub. But I will suffice with naming just a few.

The first name that pop's in is my head is Eddie, he was ex Hong Kong police. He did a good impression of Magnum before Tom Sellick got near it, in looks as well as other ways. He was a real character too, and one hell of a drinker!

Ed had a little posse of his own, his side kick was Dai Jones....yep he was Welsh! Real nice guy and also a very heavy drinker. Dai had friends too including a Welsh couple, Brian and Liz. Liz was lovely, gentle, kind and nice. Brian was a good guy too until he had a few drinks! I can remember sitting in a bar after hours , when some guy made the mistake of picking on Brian. It was like something out of a film, the guy threw a punch, Brian took him over his shoulder and put him through a table, end of fight. One of the guys friends was all for getting involved and I was raring to go when Eddie pushed me back in my seat and simply told the other guy to back off, funnily enough he did.

There were several other members of Eddie's 'gang'. One of whom was an ageing chess shop owner. Well they all seemed old to me I was in my late teens/early twenties, they were mid thirties to forties! The shop owner was a bit of a manic depressive and several years later walked in to the pub and informed everyone he had tried to shoot himself but missed. Everyone had a good laugh and told him not to be a pratt, on his part he just had a few drinks and then went home. What no one realised was that he was being serious. He did a much better attempt second time around and blew the back of his head off!

Not that I was a stranger to guns myself. When I was fourteen or so my mum and dad bought me a couple of replica pistols. And my father, a firearms expert, taught me how to use them (well in theory). Then, at the same time I started aikido I also took up small bore shooting with the NCB rifle club. I ended up with a 89% average after six months and was supposed to represent the club at a competition, but it was getting in the way of my martial arts and I dropped it.

Now where was I, oh yes, The Beehive. Other frequenters of that establishment included Robin a gay ex SAS captain and his friend and prodigy George who was known as the 'Silver Fox', due to his sly way with women and his prematurely gray hair. George was also an ex enforcer for a well known North London gang! It was George who took me under his wing for a while and introduced me to a few new clubs (normally for free as he was well known at some) and also introduced me to weight training.

So, after all that, on to possibility number two. A club. Normally we went to The Lyceum. I say we as this invariably included Neil, Dave Murphy, Tony Christopher (my best friend from secondary school), the Newcombe brothers and a couple of friends Loch and Graham.

Tony was, outside of my father, the first person I sparred with. Watching a few chop suey kung fu flicks inspired us to attempt to teach our selves kung fu (yeah I know but we were young)! Tony and I met when we were about 12/13, and we stuck together until we were about 20. Like Dave Murphy, who we had met when rescuing him from a beating by fellow attendees of Rutherford Secondary school, Tony tried his hand at aikido and like Dave ended up falling by the way side. He disappeared to find himself one day and I didn't hear from him again for about 30 years.

Club nights normally ended up with us all blind drunk. We did have a bit of a dance on the way there, sometimes even with a girl! Although it did take me several years to realise that snogging the girl before trying to hold a conversation wasn't the best course of action. One of the draw backs of an all boys school education.

On the odd occasion Dave Miller would join us, in which case the chances of 'pulling' dropped off dramatically! Much as I loved Dave as a friend and martial arts partner, he looked like a scarecrow. He had little fashion sense, wild hair and after about two pints there was half a chance he was pissed. This was not a babe magnet! That said Neil, was hardly a work of art or Dave Murphy. Phil and Jim, on the other hand, seemed quite able to pull.

And so on to the last possibility, PARTY! OK, there was good news and bad news here. Phil worked with a guy called Stuart, Stuart lived in Essex......guess where all the parties were..yep...Essex!

The parties in Essex were good and always involved a stay over at the venue or one near by. And it also expanded our social group by some margin. It also meant travelling up, normally by train, getting very pissed and regretting it the next day! Little did I realise then that I would one day head out that way to live.

Now I say Stuart and co lived in the middle of Essex, because that's how it seemed. However, in reality it was only around the Basildon area, so it wasn't so far, just seemed it for someone who was exclusively a city boy. The guys in Essex were pretty regular guys and we got on with them, and of course the girls were from Essex, so enough said!

I can remember on one occasion I went to a fancy dress party, no idea what as. While I was there I bumped in to a dishy blonde, I knew very vaguely, who was dressed as a belly dancer. We spent most of the evening horizontal on a sofa as the party went on around us. At one point I sort of noticed, out of the corner of my eye, a girl on crutches, but of course I was a bit engrossed. Until she asked if she could sit on the sofa, I didn't fancy the idea as I was happy with just me and my blonde friend on it and a little argument ensued. I had no idea that in about two or three years time the girl on the crutches would be my wife!

Chapter Four - Fights, Flights and Fiesta's

At the end of my first year (well actually just over it) I was a 3rd kyu green belt in aikido. Its not too unusual in some martial arts to get to the mid point towards a black belt in a year or two, but I was probably a little quicker than most, although by no means the fastest.

For those of you who have no idea about martial arts and the grading system, most modern martial arts use similar systems. Normally you start at red or white belt travel through yellow, orange, green, blue, brown and then on to black, known as a dan grade in Japan and duan in Chinese. There are variations with other colours being popped in arbitrarily here and then, or belts with stripes or sashes introduced, like brown belt first stripe etc.

However, the real understanding of an art or system rarely comes before black belt. When someone tells you they got to the heady heights of green belt, what they are really saying is that they are half way through the basics! But it does depend on the style and/or system. Take kung fu for instance. Wing Chuan (the style Bruce Lee started off in) is a pretty basic but effective system. It's designed to teach someone to reach a good standard quickly. Another style, like one of the shaolin systems might take 20 or 30 years to master, in the early days the Wing Chuan exponent will probably have the edge, but as time goes on and the Wing Chuan practioner hits a plateau the Shaolin exponent will continue to grow and will eventually have the edge.

Anyway as I was saying, here I was a year in and a green belt. I visited and trained with more instructor's than everyone else bar Dave Miller. And things were going well. On the mat anyway.

In other areas of my life things were not so good. I was still quite shy back then and couldn't pin down a regular girlfriend. I was drinking a lot. My mum was on my case because she thought I would end up a bit of a drunk like my dad. And I was suffering panic attacks! And of course work was crap!!

To help alleviate tensions I carried on drinking and partying. And also started to develop a bit of a mean streak when it came free style.

On a visit to George Pears club in South London I demolished the club champion in about 30 seconds. He wasn't happy, but he was a good guy and we became friends. He also had a gorgeous girlfriend, Sally! It was only later I found out that she was the sister of Sue who had started to come training at Ahmeed's classes. Sue was a nice enough girl, although a bit mad and Dave and I got on well with her. Down the line she and Dave would end up wed.

A visit by Dave and myself to one of our rival clubs was interesting. Especially when I came across another rising star. He also lasted about 30 seconds, but I nearly got thrown out of the club by the instructor Lesley, because she claimed I had done an illegal move! Such are some clubs, illegal this and illegal that, all a load of crap really. I beat her star pupil and she didn't like it. Lesley would go on to co write some well known books on Tomiki Aikido Kata with Ah Loi Lee.

Now there is a thing, not all black belts are good at fighting, actually most of them are crap at fighting. Loi is an example. Knows lots about technique and kata etc, couldn't fight for toffee, weighed about six stone soaking wet.

Aikido and Tai Chi probably boast more 'masters' and instructors who can't fight than any other systems! A shame, as both can be used wonderfully well by someone with the know how and intent.

So, when I wasn't beating up other aikidoka there were things like holidays to organise and indulge in. During my early training days in aikido (the first 6 years or so) I went on five 'martial art' holidays. The first was in my first year of training. It was the last holiday I went on with both my mum and dad. We went to Tenerife and Dave Murphy and Tony Christopher tagged along too. It wasn't too memorable but for Dave doing a great nosedive in to the Spanish dirt when we decided to do a runner from a bar. And all three of us showing off in hakama (divided skirt) and cheesy kung fu tops while practicing our aikido.

The second holiday was a little more memorable and took place in Rimini Italy. Too be honest I can't remember that much about it, but there are one or two things that stand out. This time it was me, Neil, Phil and Jim Newcombe, Graham, Loch and another guy whose name escapes me, but I didn't like him anyway. Oh I just remembered it was Ashley.

The two things that stand out are getting in to a fight and Loch 'accidentally stabbing Jim! First the fight, and how these things can grow out of nothing. There we are, a couple of drinks, down walking from one bar to another. And then I see this guy peeing against a tree. It was innocent enough, I called out 'I can see what your doing', that was it, didn't even do it in a nasty way. Of course I had to do it to the local nutter!

Before I knew what was happening there were a few words exchanged behind me and on turning around I saw the guy who had been having a pee in a heated exchange with Ashley. All of a sudden this guy grabs Ashley by the throat and, like something out of a James Bond movie, lift him off his feet with one hand and pin him against a wall! At this point I am thinking 'bugger I started this better finish it', so I yell out to the guy and tell him to let my 'mate' go.

At that point the guy drops Ashley and storms over to me, and it was then I realised how big he was. Mind you I wasn't small, six feet tall and at that time weighing about 12 stone. But he was 6'2" or 6'3" and pretty heavy built. He spoke with an accent and it later turned out he was French. So he comes over and grabs my chest and asks me if I am queer, so I push his hand away and tell him to get lost. He does it again and this time I slap his hand away with some force, it probably hurt but at the time I didn't realise that. The next instant I am trying to figure out why I can't breath and my chest feels like there is an anvil on it. Then it dawned on me he had punched me! I have never been hit so hard either before or since. But despite that I am going forward trying to swing a punch at him when suddenly the Umper lumpers arrive in force (Sorry Mr Wonker think that may be spelt wrong). By that I mean the local Italians. Turns out this guy was well known for starting fights and as soon as he threw a punch about six of the locals jumped in and grabbed us and pulled us apart. Have to admit in hindsight they were brilliant and probably stopped me from getting the first proper beating I had since I was about ten! But, the aikido had almost certainly saved me from greater injury, I was toned, used to being hit and within a few minutes I was fine.

The incident involving Loch and Jim was equally as stupid. A few nights later we are all sitting in a pizza parlour. I am sitting with Loch on my right, next to him is Jim and next to him Phil. Jim wasn't feeling too hungry and he offered his left offs to anyone who wanted them. There was an argument between Loch and Phil as to who should have what, and in the middle of Jim trying to calm things down Loch turns and points at him with his knife, well that was the idea. But in the confusion Loch just had no idea he was as close to Jim as he was and 'thud', he manages to stick the knife in Jim's neck, blood everywhere!

Now if we had been sober things might have been different. But we weren't, so Phil's reaction isn't 'oh my poor brother what can I do', its more ' I want to kill Loch but he's my mate, so I am going to kill my plate instead', and with that thumps his plate, which does a 360 degree turn as it sails about 15 feet through the air. At more or less the same time his chair does a 360 in the opposite direction. Mean while everyone is sitting there shocked, no one more so than Jim who is trying to stop the flow of blood.

Fortunately the knife had missed the main blood vessel in the neck and it looked worse than it was. Although Jim still has a pretty good scar to this day! But Phil had no idea and I think in his mind his brother could be bleeding to death and he wasn't going to stick around and watch. He stormed back to our hotel, just a hundred yards or so away and I followed him to ensure he was OK and didn't kill anyone!

On reaching his room Phil showed why a fit martial artist can be a force to be reckoned with. Having demolished his plate and chair back at the restaurant, Phil completed a hat trick with his hotel door. Now I know what your thinking, he either kicked or punched a hole in it....wrong! He wrenched the handle off, well not quite, that doesn't sound too macho until I tell you that Phil is only about 5' 8", and at the time weighed about ten stone. And that when I say he took the handle off what I actually mean is that he removed the handle and about an inch of door surrounding it as well! One thing you get in aikido is strong wrists!

Anyway, it all turned out OK in the end. Phil and Loch made up, Jim didn't bleed to death and the door got fixed the next morning and there was no charge by the hotel.

If I remember rightly the next holiday was quite

entertaining too and took place on the Norfolk Broads!
Oh yes....a boating holiday.

On the first morning of our holiday something was
missing, it was Loch, he couldn't be bothered to get up.
So that left me, Neil, Dave Murphy, Phil and Jim. Poor
boat, had no idea what it was in for!
It was a disaster from the word go or launch! Or is it
anchors away!

Anyway, within minutes of getting on board we had
buggered something up. Think it was Neil, jumped in and
smashed a side light as he did. In fact the initial light
breaking set the tone for the rest of the holiday. All in all
by the end of the week when we limped the boat back in,
we had added a few other problems.

The catalogue of disaster reads as follows. First night
we moored Jim backed our boat in to another, but no
damage done. Second night I jumped in leaned on the
windscreen as I did and it collapsed. About third day out
we raced another boat, they tried to run us in to some
reed and to avoid that I rammed them and knackered the
bow (front of the boat for those who are not nautical).
Last night we moored with the rope too loose, next
morning started off without noticing the back of the boat
was trapped under a jetty....hence no back of boat. Add
to that Phil suffering food poisoning and telling the
ambulance crew to 'fuck off' when they arrived. And Jim
taking an unexpected trip in to the broads and nearly
drowning! Apart from that it was a good holiday.

Oh nearly forgot. Also upset actor John Alterton and

wife Pauline Collins when we accidentally hit their boat while waving at them. We didn't get autographs.

There were two more 'lads' holidays after that. One in Tenerife where I encountered Kay, the girl who had been on crutches the night I had taken up the sofa with my belly dancing friend. And New York.

Up until the trip to America I think the longest flight I had done was about four hours. That said I had done a fair few by then, something in the region of 24, in a range of modern passenger jets. Some of those flights stand out more than others, especially one.

I think we were on our way back from Ibiza and got caught between two thunder storms. All the usual turbulence and a bit more. But it was the landing that really topped it off. The weather was awful, rain, fog etc. The plane came in to land and we touched down, for about two seconds and almost immediately took off again and circled around for a second attempt. Normally my dad, a crap flier who always had to get drunk to get on a plane, would have been climbing the walls, but he was so concerned with trying to calm a woman sitting opposite that he forgot about his own fear.

Anyway the approach for the second attempt at landing was like something out of a film. Children screaming, women crying. Some kid, nearby, was even saying the Lords Prayer out loud. The captain wasn't pulling any punches either. Told it as it was, diabolical conditions, one more attempt to land and if that didn't work he was hoping we had enough fuel to get to

Birmingham.

Final approach, plane pitching and rolling from side to side. Can hardly see the runway. Touch down, engines go in to reverse, breaks on......bang and the plane slides to a halt at angle of 45 degrees to the runway. One of the tires had burst on impact! Phew!!

Fortunately the trip to New York went without a hitch. However, bet you knew there would be a but, the helicopter trip over the city was interesting.

Things never go the way you expect, sometimes that's good sometimes not. Its not like the helicopter trip was a disaster or anything. There were three of us and we were just taking our first ever 'copter trip over one of the world's greatest cities. The helicopter was a run of the mill affair, although it seemed to have way too much glass for me! It held the pilot and had room for four in the back (I think) and another passenger up front next to the pilot. We piled in the back, and an American couple joined us, she sat with us while he went with the pilot.

What we didn't find out straight away was that the guy in front was the pilot's cousin and his wife was scared shitless of flying, no wonder he went up the front! It should have been a ten minute trip of us going 'oooh' 'awwwww' out of the windows. Instead it was a twenty minute trip consisting mainly of us trying to calm this poor woman down! Did see some great sights though. I just wasn't that impressed when we hit a down draft at one point and we dropped 100 feet nearer to the Empire State Building in about two seconds!

Sadly one of my best memories was going up the World Trade Centre. It hadn't been built that long and was famous as the world's tallest building as well as the thing King Kong fell off in the remake of the classic film. It had a huge impact on me in later years to watch it collapse during the terrorist attacks on it!

The trip to New York was one of those that stick in your head for years. I loved the place, loved the American people too. Did all the usual sight seeing bit's. Grahame, the same one from aikido and some of the previous holidays was working in New York for six months and we stayed in his luxury pad on 73 West Street in upper Manhattan.

He did have a different line in entertainment though. His apartment was on something like the 20th floor and overlooked another high rise across the road. When he was bored with TV he would switch all the lights out and watch the other apartment's!

OK, you got me, I called this chapter Fights, Flights and Fiestas. No Fiestas, just thought it made a good title.

Chapter Five - Coming of Age

I have given this chapter the title Coming of Age for two reasons, one because I reached 21 three years in to doing aikido. And about a year later I had another coming of age when I took my black belt grading.

But prior to both those events came a lot of training! I continued to make strides in the world of aikido in several ways. Obviously my knowledge and skills increased. I reached blue belt and then brown and was within sight of the coveted black belt. I continued to train with Irvine but also John and Ahmed and occasionally George and became good friends with all three.

I also started to attend the committee meetings which Irvine chaired and to which John was technical director. And I was given the post of licensing officer, acting as a liaison between our association and the Martial Arts Commission (MAC).

For those not old enough to remember the MAC I shall explain. The MAC was a body set up and sponsored by the government through the Sports Council. The idea was a good one, it just didn't work too well in practice. Because there were so many martial arts being taught, and because martial arts can be dangerous as well as badly taught, and as there was no overall regulation, the

MAC was invented to oversee all martial arts practiced in Britain.

For a few years the MAC did quite a good job. It vetted clubs, ensured a lot of pupils and virtually all instructors had personal liability and injury insurance. Got rid of a lot of the cowboys. And gave out official certification of rank and instructors certificates. It brought people together and it provided some good support with regard to best practice, sports injuries, first aid etc.

Had it not been for some big ego's, mainly in the karate sector, it would have continued to provide a safeguard and support for martial arts in this country. But it was a voluntary body and when several associations pulled out it collapsed.

I still have my instructors certificate for aikido from the MAC, signed by Chairman Jim Elkin. Mr Elkin was then head of our aikido rivals the BAA. Interestingly enough that honour should almost certainly have gone to our President, Rex Benlow. I only met Rex on a few occasion's, but he was everything you expected of a martial arts master. Well spoken, quite, intelligent, white hair, white beard, unassuming, you know like the old guy with the eyeballs out of 'Kung Fu'.

Rex had trained under the Japanese when they first brought aikido to this country in the 50's. When Yamada, the main man, went back to Japan he sent a letter to Rex giving him permission to set up a governing body for Tomiki aikido. The letter never got to Rex, but some how fell in to the hands of Jim Elkin who then set up the British Aikido Association, using the letter as proof of his right to do so.

Rex would have nothing to do with the BAA and therefore along with some other senior figures set up the Aikido Development Society. This association still exists today and at the time of writing is run by Don Bishop, who will feature later in this narrative.

As luck would have it I came across a website for the ADS while researching for this book. It made quite interesting reading, especially the bit where the history of the ADS was totally rewritten by someone. There was no mention of Rex, Irvine, his brother Peter or any other number of people who ran it and ensured its continuance during the 70's. In fact the site had it being founded about 20 years after it was and the two founders were named as Don Bishop and Ahmeed Saeed. As you will know by know, Ahmeed back then was a junior dan grade (he was still first dan when I met him, where as Rex was 3rd, as was Irvine and John and George both 2nd) and Don had yet to turn up on the scene.

Anyway all that aside. In 1976 I turned 21!! So how did a responsible up and coming martial artist celebrate his coming of age. Dressed up like a turnip and went to a strip club of course! Well when I say a turnip, I don't mean as in fancy dress, well that's arguable. I went out in a three piece pinstripe suit with a Fedora hat. There were quite a few of us, Tony, Dave Murphy, Dave Miller, Phil, Jim, Loch, Grahame, Terry, Neil and a few more. Started in the pub in Victoria, The Talbot. And ended up in a club in Soho.

The club was interesting for a few reasons, for a start it was seedy in the extreme, you could bunk in the back door, so we didn't pay and it didn't have a dance license......Umm.yep you did hear right, no dance license and it was a strip club. They got round it by having a small stage with a curtain. The stripper would come on clothed and strike a pose, which she would then hold for about a minute. The curtain would come down and when it went back up she would have moved and removed a bit of clothing too! It was almost as bad as watching paint dry. But we all sat down the front and while she was holding her pose we struck up a conversation with her, which didn't make the management too happy.

Needless to say got home very drunk, woke up with a hang over and yet another promise to never drink again, which lasted to that evening. And life rolled on.

By this time Dave Miller and Sue had been going out for some time and the day came when I was reading out the telegrams as best man at their wedding. It was one of those occasions when everyone seemed to be there. Dave's mum and dad had come down from Scotland, a great couple. When I had stayed at their home in Edinburgh Dave's dad, Sandy, had spent two weeks verbally abusing me, in good jest of course. A real funny guy but a pretty hard man too.. But , at the end of the day, the man I considered one of my best friends was now a married man!

In those early days my life was not totally dedicated to

aikido, believe it or not. In amongst the boozing and aikido I also manage to fit in Tae Kwon Do and later on a bit of Iaido and Jodo and a little bit of Spirit Combat.

Phil started to go to a Tae Kwon Do club in South London and I tagged along. This was back in the days when men were men (well some), and doing very silly things wasn't frowned on. So we did things like run circuits of the church hall where we trained. Easy you may think, not when its a gravel car park outside and you are in bare feet though. It's also not so funny when you do press ups on your knuckles and discover there is broken glass amongst the gravel too.

For those reader's who are not familiar with Tae Kwon Do it is a Korean martial art, often called Korean karate. It originated in the 50's but its roots go back thousands of years. These days the difference between it and karate is minimal as they have both borrowed so much from each other. Primarily Tae Kwon Do ripped Karate off for its kata and Karate ripped off all the high kicks.

Many people, including many karateka, don't realise that back as recently as 50's and even 60's, the system didn't have many high kicks. Nearly all the more dynamic kicks used in karate now come from Tae Kwon Do.

More people may be aware of Tae Kwon Do now that it is part of the Olympics'. Sadly, like so many good martial arts, what you see at the Olympics' is not really representative of what the art is really about. When you turn any martial art in to a sport you lose far more than you gain. Take boxing for instance. Up until the Marquis of Queensbury brought in his rules boxing was not a million miles away from many other martial arts. It had throw's as well as punching applications and it could be used as a solid self defence method. But as soon as the rules came in and the restrictions on target areas and the use of punches only was enforced, it lost it's effectiveness as a real combat system. Anyone trying to use boxing only as a basis for self defence would get a serious beating from any competent martial artist or street fighter.

The club I attended was not part of the organisation which supplies competitors at the Olympic games. And the sort of Tae Kwon Do they taught was more orientated to street fighting than impressing a judge. Hardly surprising, considering two out of the three instructors were ex army. And the club would eventually fold because army guys left for pastures new, in one case that included reenlisting as well!

I only did Tae Kwon Do for a year. But it did open my eye's to the benefits of other martial arts and I was never totally happy with just Aikido after that, because, like most systems of combat, it was not complete.

As mentioned earlier John France practiced Jodo and Iaido as well as Aikido. I was lucky that he was prepared to instruct me in both, on a one to one basis, for about 18 months. Although I never went in for official gradings in either, he rated me as about a 1st kyu brown belt in both. And they certainly helped my Aikido practice, which, of course includes the bo (a shorter version of the jo) and the sword.

One of the guys who attended class turned out to be a pupil of one Brian Dossett. For a lot of martial artists this name will be familiar, although it tends to get a mixed reaction!

Brian started his combat career as a prize fighter in a fair, taking on all comers. There is no denying the guy was hard and could take a punch as well as deliver one. He studied Karate and Ju Jutsu as well as other systems and attained several black belts. And at that point drove a very big wedge between certain sectors of the martial arts community. Some people think he is a genius while others look on him as a heretic. Why? Because he started his own martial art. These days it's advertised as based on Ju Jutsu but incorporating elements from aikido, Kung Fu, boxing and Karate. But for many people back then it was a totally new martial art. I also think that some of his breaking exploits pissed a few people off, if not frightened them. He used to do things like take the top off of several free standing bottles with the edge of his hand, or head butt telegraph poles in half!

Today Brian is well accepted in some areas but still seen as having tinkered too much with traditional teachings by others. I can only speak as I found him back then. He was a nice guy, worked hard and was hard. I trained with him several times but due to my training for my black belt in Aikido I never took up Spirit Combat seriously.

In 1978 I finally got to go for the big prize, my first dan. By that time the set up in our little Aikido circle had changed a bit. Rex Benlow had taken a back seat and a few new instructors and clubs had joined the fold. One of the new instructors was Don Bishop.

Today Don runs the Aikido Development Society, back then he was just coming back in to the fold having been running his own independent club for some time. He was known to the likes of Irvine, and especially John France, as Don had been his original instructor. John was never the same after Don arrived, there was bad blood between them, and he marginalised himself more and more. He even went as far as moving to the practice of Yoshinkan Aikido, a different style and affiliating to a new instructor. Although the guy turned out to be a bit of a fraud which in turn soured John's view of Aikido.

When Don arrived on the scene he was a 3rd dan. But with Irvine's job keeping him from regular practice and John France stepping down as Technical Director, Don took over but convinced the board of dan grades that to do so he should be graded to 4th dan. Which they did by a vote.

Anyway, that aside, my black belt grading was arranged for a Thursday evening at the NCB club and it would be jointly overseen by Irvine and Don. It was a pretty big thing as in the previous fours years there had been only two or three other dan gradings. And of those people graded to black I would only be Irvine's second pupil to get that far and by far the youngest too.

On the night all the usual faces were there, Dave Miller, Dave Murphy, Phil and Jim etc. Plus several students from other clubs attended. And, to my delight, my father!

It was not an easy grading! We did the warm up's, break fall practice, movement practice. Bit of kata. Then I got called up to perform my first kata, I would get called up four times to perform kata, including the first 24 moves of the Dai San which included knife attacks. In total about 64 separate techniques with three or four different partners.

Intermixed amongst the kata was kakari geiko, the practice where one of you attacks and one defends and then you swap. Free movement, a sort of continuous relaxed sparring and then the biggie! I had to take on two of Don's guys who got to attack me with knifes. It wasn't expected and I was not going to take prisoners. I nearly broke one of the guys ankles when I threw him and they didn't touch me at all!

After all that I had to pick a technique of my choice and teach it to the class, and that included the black belts grading me. We finished, as normal, with a warm down and meditation.

At the end of the session I was called out and Irvine tied my black belt around my waist. I have had few prouder moments. Everyone gathered around to shake my hand and pat me on the back and then I went to my father who was standing there with tears in his eyes. I don't think he ever thought he would see the day, it was one of the few times I can remember him hugging me. Needless to say, after that we all went to the pub!

Chapter Six - Wedding Bells

In the next couple of years Dave Miller, Phil and Jim all collected their black belts too. The BBC club moved from Putney to Covent Garden and sadly Irvine informed us he was going to leave Britain and join his brother in Australia.

As it was, quite soon after the grading I was running a lot of the classes myself as Irvine was still having trouble getting to class. It was during one of these sessions I lost my front teeth. Between my dentist, Irvine, sweets and bad luck I had already lost a fair bit of them as it was. But Phil's foot sealed the deal! I would love to relate how it was done during a fight or sparring, but it was actually a total accident when we were warming up. We were doing wheel barrows as part of a warm up session and I had Phil's right ankle in my hand and all he had to do was kick up his left for me to grab. He didn't, I bent forward to grab it and at that point he swung it up straight in to my mouth, bang, no front teeth! Well, mostly no teeth, just enough for two crowns.

One of the guys training opposite our area in Covent Garden was Dan Docerty. Dan was famous for winning the South East Asian open martial arts division. He was a Karate man when he went to Hong Kong as a police officer. While there he learned Tai Chi Chuan. On returning to Britain he took up teaching Wudang Tai Chi full time. At that time he was one of the few people in this country to teach 'proper' Tai Chi including combat application. Little did I know then that I would later compete in one of his competitions.

Irvine upped and left for Australia, a sad day. I was left to run his clubs along with Phil and Dave Miller.

At work I managed to get a promotion, and I left the NCB headquarter behind Buckingham Palace, for smaller offices just off of Fleet Street. Just as well considering all the problems there had been when the miners had picketed the place. I also left behind what I had seen as the potential love of my life, one Susan Smith. If only she had felt the same, but she didn't. All I had been was a constant irritation in the office we had worked in together.

My new job wasn't taxing in the least and I found myself disappearing to the pubs near The Temple more often than not. I got friendly with some of the guys there and got involved with a few football matches between departments and played a bit of table tennis. I had never been good at either, but I certainly improved a far deal. Did I mention I was an Arsenal Supporter? If I didn't I am.

In late 1979 I went on holiday to Tenerife again with the Essex mob. The usual suspects were there, Stuart or Mr Status Quo, as I thought of him, one of the groups biggest fans. Andy, big guy, Tae Kwon Do black belt. Paul, could write a book about him and will enlighten you more later. Steve Burr and Steve Fewtrell, two good guys we had met on a previous holiday along with Chris Fulford, who would go on to be a fairly successful actor.

As I said earlier Kay was on that holiday. She actually went with her long term boyfriend. But things were on the wane and we got on well too. Within a couple of weeks of coming back there was a party and unbeknown to me Kay had ditched her boyfriend and was asking around to see if I was going to this party.

Not too surprising then that she made a beeline for me when I arrived. And we ended up staying the night, even if she was in a camper and I was laying below it.

Kay was a pretty girl, intelligent, positive and overweight! In the years we were together she went from pleasantly plump to down right fat and back again, several times. But she had an infectious personality, was a natural mother figure (even though her only child, which she had at 16, was adopted) and was open minded and loved to socialise.

It was more or less love at first sight and within five months we were married. My mother was not impressed, probably with good reason.

Apart from the fact Kay was my first long term girlfriend. She was, as I said, fat and at times quite loud, my mother liked neither. Also I jacked in my long term job at the NCB in. We had this idea about spending some time on a kibbutz with Stuart and Steve Burr. So my mother blamed that on Kay too.

1980 was a big year, and not for all the right reasons. Kay and I married early in the year in Grays Registry office Essex. The reception was at her mum and dad's in Corringham. They were a nice couple, although a bit yokel, prudish, and very close. Kay's dad did all the catering.

My father and mother attended but my father was obviously not well and at one point fell of his seat. He spent some time laying down in one of the bedrooms. He had been off work for a couple of years due to a hip problem caused in an accident. During that time it had become more and more difficult for him to walk and he had lost a lot of weight.

The wedding and the meal after went well. And in the evening we had a party with Kay's family and our friends from Essex. My sister in law Denise and her husband attended too.

We flew out to Tunisia for our honeymoon, staying in a brand new five star hotel. It was nice although a little quiet. And I got offered two camels for my new wife, by one of the market traders! I didn't take him up on the offer as I couldn't think of where to put two camels!

When we got back we stayed with my mum while waiting for the kibbutz plan to take off. While there one evening we were sitting on the sofa watching TV, my mum was in the kitchen, when my dad came down from the bedroom, he looked terrible, yellow, gaunt, he was only in underpants and clearly had no idea where he was.

I will always remember the look on his face, he look like a startled and very frightened bush baby. Suddenly he half leaned half fell back and at the same time he lost control of his bladder and pissed himself, it was orange!

I had no idea what to do. I called for my mother who, initially, lost her temper, but then realised my father wasn't himself at all. We managed to get him on the sofa and my mother phoned for medical assistance.

Now comes the hard bit, because I have to confess to several stupid, and on the face of it callous mistakes on my part. I look back now and see how weak and confused and deluded I was. If it's any consolation to my family, friends and you the reader, I have to admit to being haunted by the whole episode, and probably will be to the day I die.

I didn't want to be around the situation, here was a man who had scared me, fascinated me, educated me, amused me and finally befriended me man to man. But he wasn't that man, he was a withered worn out shell and I hated it. I had seen him go down hill for years and it hurt to watch it. And now finally this, I couldn't take it. So Kay and I went out and left my poor mother too it. I consoled myself with the fact she was strong, had the matter in hand and we were in the way.

As we left my father was stretched out on the sofa apparently asleep. I called out 'bye' to my mother and heard my father slur 'see you', it was the last thing he ever said to me and the last time I saw him.

In my mind he was dead, I had seen my beloved grandmother go the same way when I was just 18 and she was only 66. I knew he was going to die. Over the next two weeks my mother visited him in hospital and each time she came back it was to report that he had no idea who he was or when it was. Apparently at times he thought he was back in the navy. I have no idea if this was the result of illness or medication or both, but it was a carbon copy of how my grandmother had been. I couldn't face seeing him and convinced myself that visiting him would be wrong for a number of reasons.

A couple of weeks later I got up and went down to the kitchen to find my mother at the sink. She simply turned and said ' your fathers dead', we both burst in to tears and hugged. He had been just 50 years old.

Stupidity was compounded on the day of the funeral when I didn't go. I hated the church and all the crap it stood for. And refused to stand around while someone who didn't even know my father came out with a pile of shit. Moreover I had a chest infection and had been told by my doctor to stay indoors. So I did.

That silly decision cost me friends from the Beehive and alienated me from my mother for six months. Soon after the funeral Kay and I went to stay at her parents. We never did get to the Kibbutz, although Steve and Stuart went. And I didn't go to aikido for about eight months. It was the end of the line for a lot of things, life would never be the same again.

Chapter Seven - Essex Boy

I was an Essex boy now, albeit an unemployed one living with his in laws! But with pressure on both Kay and I to find a job and our own place we were both soon commuting up to London on a regular basis.

Kay managed to get herself a job doing accounts near Fenchurch Street. While I landed a job with the British Library as a clerk. Neither were mind boggling positions, but they did pay a wage. And initially I had the good fortune to be working at the British Museum, a place I had always loved.

After a couple of silly letters and a couple of phone calls I had patched things up with my mother, and eventually I took the time to pop back and see her. She hadn't been idle. Despite avoiding the pub scene in my earlier years she had in my father's later years, started to join him for a drink most evenings. It had been nice to see them out together after so many years of separation and bad feeling, and it was kind of cool to be able to bump in to my both mum and dad in the boozer sometimes.

Since my father's death my mother had continued to go to the pub and had met a guy called Bob Rayner. By the time I popped in to see her Bob had moved in and they were living together. The first meeting was a bit odd and I think we were both very wary and unsure of each other.

Bob was nothing like my dad, and at something like 15 years my mum's junior wasn't even older enough to be my father. He was short with dark longish hair and tubby. He worked for London Underground as an escalator engineer. He had been married before and already had several kids of his own too.

All that said he seemed a nice enough guy. And indeed he was. And he obviously idolised my mum. My mum and Bob would eventually marry and he would go on to be the best step father anyone could wish for.

Once I was back at work and earning some money I could go back to Aikido. But things had changed there in my absence and Phil had started to run things. Even the style had changed a bit and we were now affiliated to Shodakan Aikido with a direct link to 7th dan, and head of the system, Sensie Nariyama. He visited Phil's new club and helped establish the spin off from Tomiki Aikido in this country. I was one of the founder members of the style in the UK, but to be honest I found some of the new techniques and the more sporty approach less appealing than the system we had trained in before.

There is no denying Nariyama is a skill martial artist and a nice guy. And he had the full backing of Tomiki to set up his system. But it just wasn't for me. For those of you who are now thinking 'doesn't he mean Shotokan Karate', no I don't! Shodokan is the latest mutation of one of the branches of Aikido.

Like many martial arts before it, Aikido has undergone several transformations, and like many other systems these transformations often co exist. It's a bit like driving down the road and spotting an Aston Martin DB6, you know that prior to the DB6 there was a DB5 and so on and since the DB6 there has been a DB7,8,9 etc. Of course the latest model will have all the mod cons on it and people will expect it to be the best thing since sliced bread. But some people will argue that an earlier model was faster, or more reliable, or looked better. It's the same with martial arts.

In the case of Aikido Uyeshiba took elements from several systems he had practiced, including Daito Ryu Aiki Jutsu, and formulated something new. Notice I say new, not better. Having produced this new 'art', he went on to teach other people, including several high ranking martial artist's like Gozo Shioda and Kenji Tomiki. They then took elements of the system and developed it again, thus producing a new sub system. And in Nariyama's case he took the Tomiki system and twisted again to produce Shodokan Aikido.

Karate did the same, and there are now many styles of Karate from Shotokan, considered by many to be the base style to one's yet to be named and still being worked out by enthusiastic black belts. Kung Fu can probably boast that it has more variations on a theme than any other martial art and the styles run in to the hundreds and maybe even thousands.

The big difference these days is you often get people

setting up styles and claiming that their system is the best and is so totally new all the old styles look silly in comparison. You only have to look at some of the schools that have been set up to feed the need for mixed martial arts styles required by aspiring cage fighters. Although they often have a claim to legitimacy that many, so called modern, martial artists don't have, they can prove if their style works in fairly realistic conditions. There are a lot of 'modern masters', who have never had a real fight, yet claim their new system is the 'dogs bollocks'! At least the older styles and systems can often boast that they have been proved in real combat, in some cases to the death!

So Phil did me a favour, and in return I didn't rock the boat. He had had an offer to run an evening class in a school near Kings Cross. So he got it up and running and then handed it over to me. I ran that class for over ten years on my own.

It is a scary thing to branch out by yourself and teach everything from scratch. Taking over Irvine's classes had been fairly easy, everything was in place and most of the students already established in what they were learning. The Islington Adult Education presented me with over 30 students one evening and left me to it. Only a couple of them had had any martial arts training before.

I based my classes closely on how I had been taught by Irvine, but as time progressed and the students started to grasp the concept of Aikido I brought other elements in that I had learned with Ahmed and John. And at the end of the first year I still had a dozen students training, most of whom continued in to the second year.

Amongst some of my students were a few who showed promise. James was one. He had foreign blood of some sort, although I never did get to the bottom of what it was, by his look, he was short but fairly stocky with black hair and a square face, I thought it have been Polynesian blood. His youngest son Vince also attended class. He was only about sixteen when he started but he had a problem I had never come across before, he only had the one leg! He had been born with only a stump and had learned to walk with an artificial leg from an early age. Considering the restrictions he had he managed to more than keep up with other people in the class and eventually got his green belt before he left to go to university. His dad stayed with me for a number of years and ended up as a brown belt. Unfortunately there is a bad ending to my association with James and Vince.

I think Vince had been at uni for just under a year when James came to see me and give me some bad news. He and one of his other sons had gone to visit Vince and they had gone for a drive. Somehow the car had gone off the road and flipped over several times before coming to a halt. Because of his leg Vince normally would have occupied the front seat and been wearing a seatbelt but for once he had gone in the back, in the days when rear seatbelts were not compulsory. He had been thrown from the car as it rolled and the car had landed on him and killed him instantly. Obviously we were all devastated, no one more than his father, who I think blamed himself for the accident. James was never the same man after that. And a few years later when a proposed business deal, which would have seen us running a gym come martial arts centre, folded our friendship folded too.

I had other students who stayed with me longer than James, Rob was one. Rob turned up with beard and a ponytail and a tale of having been out of work for a while. He was one of life's less successful characters and he knew it. But he stuck with me for years, eventually getting his second dan and was my leading student. By the time we finished with him the hair was cut, beard gone, he was employed as a carpenter and had a much more positive and outgoing demeanour. I can't say it was all down to me, but I certainly didn't hinder his progress. I still have a sword stand he made for me.

Another one of my early students was John, he had done a little Karate and decided to give Aikido a shot. He also got to black belt and was a regular for some years.

One of my big successes was Eric. Eric was tall, gangly, inept and didn't pick up techniques terribly well but he too got to black belt in the end. As did Graham, a far more practical type and ex TA soldier. When I finally finished with the club I left it in their hands.

In all over the years I graded one person to second dan and five to first dan. But of all those people who trained under me one stood out, and at times for all the wrong reasons.

Noel Reece turned up one night to class, early in the second year of me running the adult education classes.

Noel is one of those larger than life characters who is always ready to make a new friend. He stands about 5'10", stocky build, big nose, gray hair, a few tats and nearly always a big grin. Back in those days he more often than not turned up in motorcycle leathers, for Noel loves bikes, which, is hardly surprising for an ex Hell's Angel!

Noel is one of those guys who throw's himself in to things and that's what he did both in class and afterwards when we went for a quick drink. Most people took to him straight away, but of course there are always a couple of exceptions. And Noel can be loud. Noel also didn't mess around on the mat. And that could have upset one or two people too.

Unlike a lot of martial arts students Noel was a fairly accomplished street fighter, and I couldn't use that in the past tense back then either. After me spending hours on the mat and in the pub trying to instil a certain chivalry in my students, that old samurai code. Noel would turn up eyes downcast and standing on the edge of the mat, telling me he had better not attend class that day as he had let the side down. In other words he had had a fight and beaten the crap out of someone. I rarely turned him away though as it was often six of one and half a dozen of the other, and he had just done what a lot of people wanted to but were just too scared to.

Noel stayed with the class for a number of years and got to brown belt. But he has remained one of my best friends ever since and we still see as much of each other as we can. It's a shame I can't spend more time on Noel in this book, but I would hardly do justice to him as he probably merits a whole book by himself!

Kay and I had been married for about a year when, with some help from my mother, we managed to secure a mortgage on a three bedroom flat in Finches Close Coringham, only a ten minute walk from her mum and dad's! It was the beginning of real married life and proper freedom. But it came with a price. At 17,500.00 the flat was then, a reasonable price but still the mortgage took up half our wages, add to that the train fares and bus fares and it's not difficult to see why, at the end of some months we were reduced to eating beans on toast for dinner!

But things could have been worse and our friends popped around on a regular basis, sometimes a little too regular! Considering we were newly married and newly living alone we very rarely were. Not that we complained much, late night drinking sessions, silly games and deep conversations on anything from the occult through politics and on to sex made life more than interesting.

We got our selves a cat. Well really it was more like helping it out. It was a stray that we took in and like idiots we thought lets get it a friend and purchased a kitten to keep it company. Big mistake as Blackie (who was tabby) hated Scrabble (who was black) on sight. And then to top it off Blackie got pregnant and gave birth to Wriggley. Three cats and we hadn't been sold on one to start.

Steve and Stuart finally returned from the Kibbutz, Steve having Debbie, a girl from Bradford now in tow.

And then another one of the crowd, Paul Newing, purchased a flat just a couple of doors down from us. Eventually another friend, Willy, would also buy one of the other flats too.

With three of 21 flats occupied by our crowd, Stuart only just around the corner and several other members of the gang as regular visitors it wasn't long before we had come to the attention of the local police with some of our silly antics! To be honest most of it was just fun and weren't malicious, just a bit thoughtless and daft. But things did get quite amusing on a few occasions. There was, for instance, the water fight incident.

After yet another fun filled evening in the local Stuart, Paul, myself and a couple of others ended up back in Paul's flat. Paul, for some reason I have never fathomed, decided to start a water fight. It got just a little out of hand and saw us all half clothed and wringing wet, as was most of the flat! Just as we reached the height of the fun I noticed a blue flashing light somewhere below. Of course we went in to stealth mode, which for us, in the state we were in, consisted of turning the lights off and shsshing each other in stage whispers. As this was going on the letterbox flap slowly lifted and a male voice informed us that our shsshing could be heard! It was just one of a number of times the police would pop round to see if we were alright.

On another occassion Paul had a toga party that rivalled anything from the movie Animal House. Kay wasn't too well that night and mainly stayed at our place. But her friend Jan decided that she should keep Kay company for some of the time.

Jan was, in those days, one of those head turners. Blond, buxom, attractive and very out going. One of those girls who walked in at a party and everyone wanted to pull. And she wasn't afraid to be pulled either.

On this particular occasion Jan turned in toga as expected. But as maybe not expected minus any underwear what so ever! A fact I noticed as she rolled around on our living room floor playing with the cats (we had two back then, although two multiplied in to three, strange as they were both female)?! Later, while Kay sat watching TV I helped Jan adjust her Toga, well that's how it started! It was the start of a little cat and mouse game which never quite went all the way.

Hardly surprising but at 24 and with little previous experience of women I was very much up for everything and anything. And the Jan incident only heralded more interest and several risky 'games'. One such game saw us all swap partners for the night! The idea was just a platonic sleep in but I am sure half the people involved were hoping for more. I got a girl called Cheryl and she certainly got more than she expected.

As time moved on more of our friends paired off and married. One of these pairs were Steve and Dawn. They married and moved in to a house in the very new town of South Woodham Ferries in darkest Essex.

We often went over to them or they came to us for drinks and meals. And it wasn't long before we played some silly games with them, like strip poker, well actually it was strip cribbage, just as much fun, just a lot slower! But again we stopped just short of going all the way. Although we did go all the way....to Corfu with them on holiday.

But, not long after taking up residence in South Woodham Steve joined a martial art's club, and was soon waxing lyrical about Ju Jutsu. Of course it wasn't long before I had to give it a go.

Me aged about 18 outside our flat in Ashmill Street and below

Mum and dad on holiday in Tenerife

Me at blue belt in aikido throwing Dave Miller

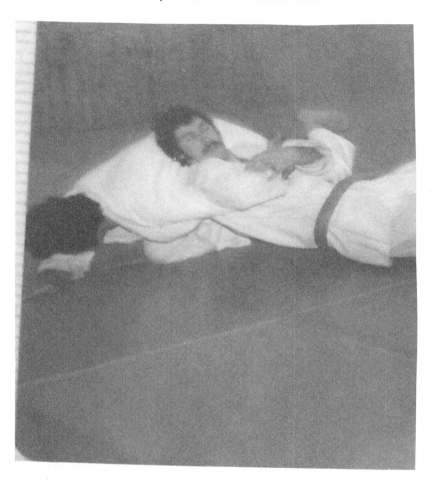

Me forcing Ahmed Saeed to the ground during aikido randori

Sensie Irvine Cleydon at a demo about to throw Tony Harper

Me doing Tae Kwon Do

Sensie Nariyama

Me doing a Ju jutsu display Sensie Devlin in the background

Me during my bodybuilding phase with top bodybuilder Berry DeMay

Sensie Inoue of the Hontai Yoshin Ryu

Sensie Terry Parker

First PCSO's on Redbridge with Grahame Clark and the Mayor

With my friend Colin Dunn (European kick boxing champ) playing in 'Grease'

Noel Reece and myself at my wedding to Trish

Trish and I at our wedding or rather leaving it

Me and the boys

Luke performing at Sifu's birthday celebrations

Sifu and Simu with the first UK disciples back row left to right -Dong, Spencer, Ting, Me, Ed, Kevin, Gary front row - Simu and Sifu

Ed and I having just won the European two man event

Ed and I during our weapons form at the Europeans

And that wonderful moment with Alex 'threatening' if we won any more medals......

Sifu Lu performing in America 2008

Sifu's father Lu Zhen Dou warming up

Trish and I at Greenwich Uni for my Certificate in Education award

Me with dadoe winning gold at world championships

And another of me in Shanghai

Me with Xante Bearman BBC Radio Essex

Some of the other guys performing -

Adam Lynch and Andy Lee

Kevin Kilminster

Andy Denny

Errol Armstong

Gary Matthews

Ed Hutton

Me and Luke at British championships 2012 - two

man silver medal

Me and the family at my passing out ceremony

The Jow ga Institute in the USA Sifu's Hon and Reza sit either side of Sifu Lu

Kevin and I doing Tai Chi

Sifu and Hon Lee

Chapter Eight - Forget the Do give me a Jutsu

I took to ju jutsu like a duck to water. It had everything I wanted out of a martial art and included many elements I felt had been squeezed out of aikido.

The club I started at was run by a guy called Brian Devlin, ex army, hard as nails and a great guy. He wasn't a big man but he packed a punch and was all heart! In some cases quite literally. Like, for instance, when he had open heart surgery one Thursday and was taking the class again the following Thursday! Brian was what I term a real martial artist, someone who wasn't afraid to get stuck in and take a little pain as well as dish it out. And someone you really didn't want a fight with. But he had a good sense of humor and was always keen to help.

He ran his club with a firm hand and was happy to drive people to exhaustion to get that bit more from them. And he lead by example.

Brian had originally studied Goshin Ryu style ju jutsu but at that time was under Terry Parker banner and taught jukka Ryu. But he still retained certain elements of his previous system that he passed on to his students.

Terry was an older and apparently softer exponent of the fighting arts. But looks could be deceiving! Terry was, back then, about mid fifties and a sixth dan in ju jutsu. He was, outside of London, the main man in the South for the British Ju Jutsu Association. And he was successful enough to go full time as a martial arts instructor when I knew him. He was one of those charismatic people who you wanted to like and do things for. And along with Brian he became my main ju jutsu sensie.

The thing about ju jutsu is that unlike some martial arts it retains its essence as a fighting art, an effective and at times very violent one at that. It was ju jutsu that Jigaro Kano took and used as his template for modern judo. But judo is so shorn of techniques and content as to be only a pale shadow of the complete martial art ju jutsu is.

In the days of the Samurai, before karate, aikido and judo, there was only ju jutsu. But there were thousand's of school's each one different to the next. Some of these schools still survive and in some cases have given birth to more modern systems as well. Ju jutsu , as I said, is a complete art. It includes throws, locks, strikes, kicks, nerve holds, chokes, strangles, etc etc. Techniques are practiced standing, kneeling and laying down. When ever I am asked by someone 'what martial art should I do for self defense', even now I still say ju jutsu. That's not because its the most successful system or complicated, but because for the average person it's the one they will get to grips with and be able to use for real the easiest!

Jukka Ryu Ju Jutsu came to Britain by way of the States. To be honest there didn't seem to be much history to it, other than Ju Jutsu had gone to America and at some point Jukka Ryu had grown up out of it as a separate style. However as I progressed in the style I did learn that it's main claim to fame was it's practitioner's being able to take a hit. I once saw some footage of one of the American masters taking a three way simultaneous strike to the neck and throat by black belts who had just proved their ability to smash boards and bricks. It was quite funny watching him walk away unhurt while one of the guys studied his fist trying to figure out what had gone wrong. The other thing that became apparent was that on moving from America to the UK there had been the introduction of elements Preying Mantis kung fu in to the system.

Although I was doing Ju jutsu Thursday's, then Saturday's and Sunday's I still kept my aikido class going too. In fact as I realized how some of the aikido techniques had been watered down I started to incorporate some of my ju jutsu in to the aikido classes.

It was not long before my aikido had a definite ju jutsu flavour to it. And the more I learned the more I realised how aikido had lost it's way. For some aikido goes beyond martial arts and embraces cosmic love and unity. But, as a martial art some aspects of it seriously sucked, and now I could see why! Time and again I saw how an effective fighting technique had been reduced to a shadow of it's former self. And so the 'do' of my system gave way to the jutsu of a more serious fighting art.

Over the next few years I trained hard and pushed on to purple belt. I learned sweeps, hip throws, wheel throws, shoulder throws, arm locks, ankle locks, head locks, chokes, strangles, how to fight blind folded, how to fight with one arm and a lot more. And I became a member of the Southern Area Display team.

I enjoyed being part of the display team, because unlike some of the displays I had been involved with before they were diverse, well thought out and quite often funny as well as dramatic! Terry normally opened the display's with a little speech and a few moves to set the scene. He would often say something like, 'and today you will see strikes', and with that someone would jump up and rush him only to be felled by a well aimed punch or chop. He would then go on to throw someone, then lock them up and finally would suggest the audience might see a few unusual techniques, and with that someone would grab him in a bear hug from behind. Terry would slip a hand back and apparently grab his assailants groin, the hapless attacker and would groan and sag and Terry would walk away as he threw two ping pong balls in the air, normally to quite a round of laughter from the spectators. The one thing you never saw Terry do was hit the floor, he had broken his back as a stuntman and risked being paralysed if he did a break fall!

As I had a reasonable knowledge of sword techniques, and Terry was happy to use my 'expertise'. I taught one of the other guys a few moves which we showcased at some of the demo's. It went down quite well, especially when we made the occasional cock up. Like the time my partner mixed moves up. I was expecting a downward cut to my hand and he went to a straight lunge to my midriff. Fortunately I saw it at the last second and dodged to one side, just as well as we were using live blades! A huge cheer went up from the crowd and we got a good round of applause, it was only afterward that I found a hole going straight through my gi, he had missed impaling me by only an inch or so!!

Off the mat things were ticking along too. Most of our friends were married or at least paired off. My sister in law left her husband and took up with another guy. Kay changed jobs and was doing OK. And we moved from Corringham to Basildon and in to a three bedroom house with a huge garden and just minutes from the town center. And I left the British Library and moved in to the local DHSS (Department for Health and Social Security).

But we didn't last long in Basildon nor did I last long at the DHSS. It was after all just another boring government job and I wanted more. And so I got myself a job as a manager of a newsagents in Dagenham.

Little did I realise it was the beginning of the end for Kay and me. Things went badly from the start. We sold our house and moved in to the flat above the shop in Lodge Avenue just off of the A13.

The very small minded people who lived there before us took anything and everything, even the light bulbs!

The flat was OK though, garden was a mess and the shop small and unexciting. And I had to get up at silly O clock to open it and take the papers in!

Part of the deal was Kay being assistant manager, so she had to give up her job. And to be fair it really wasn't her thing one little bit!

But the good news was there was a Ju Jutsu club run by Terry Parker just around the corner and not long after I moved to Dagenham he also opened up another club in Barking. But to be honest I didn't enjoy my training as much with a new bunch of people. Of course I knew some of them, but it just wasn't the same.

However, getting in to London for my aikido class was a bit easier now. And although I had left the evening classes and gone private I still had a good hardcore of students.

My way of doing aikido had migrated away from how I had done it under my old instructors. Don't get me wrong, they were good and knowledgeable. But they also subscribed in part or whole to a limited attack and response. And it was something I could not continue in good faith.

In my class during free practice any attack could be used from a punch to a kick, grabs, charges, head locks, bear hugs, all of them were legal. And because of that my students had no preconceived
ideas of what an attack may be.

One of my students was a French guy who had done kung fu to reasonable standard and when we fought he did like to put the occasional sweep in, which was awkward but taught me a lot. He had held the position of enforcer at his kung fu club, a position I also held at ju jutsu.

For those not in the know, an enforcer did things the instructor
couldn't do for a whole plethora of reasons. But they included things like taking on challenges from visiting martial artist's and keeping unruly students inline.

To be honest I didn't have a huge amount to do as enforcer and it was all very unofficial anyway. But Terry did use me a couple of times, including the time one of the black belts took his wife out in a big way (as in threw her hard, nothing sexual). I simply got the 'teach him a lesson' chat and happily bounced him off the floor a few times until he had had enough.

One of the things about ju jutsu is you have to be fit to really get good at it. And boy did we get put through our paces. Each lesson we did about a hundred or so break falls, plus loads of kicks, punches, sit ups, press ups etc etc. And, by the time you were going for brown belt you had learned about 200 techniques.

I did my brown belt under Professor Morris 10th Dan. I was a long and arduous session and half way through I had to go off to be sick and nearly didn't come back. It was only Terry's missus who talked me in to doing the rest of the grading, but I did pass.

During my time with the ju jutsu crowd we did a few seminars, including visiting the Mecca of British ju jutsu up in Liverpool and training under Professor Clark 10th Dan. However the highlight of these get together's was the visit from Soke Inoue, then head of the Hontai Yoshin Ryu, Japan's oldest surviving school of ju jutsu. And it was he who awarded me a second dan in aiki jutsu for my dedication and time devoted to both aikido and ju jutsu.

Chapter Nine - Out on the Street

While working as manager of the Newsagents I had various paperboys and papergirls working under me. Two of these were a brother and sister, Barry and Anjali. They were a little more reliable than some and also happy to take on extra duties and along with some of the other kids we got quite friendly.

The kids even did a few little party tricks, like when one of them moved my car (with the help of my wife Kay) and then told me it had been towed and I had to make my way to Barking Police Station to recover it. When I got there the little dears were all there to wish me a happy April Fool's day. My car was actually just around the back of the shop! Oh I did laugh....and they could all run faster than me anyway!

Anyway, over the following months Kay hated the job more and more and I got closer and closer to Anjali. And before anyway picks up the phone to call the police, she was 16, going on 17 at this point, although I was now approaching 32.

To cut a long story short Kay and I sat down one day

and decided it was over. We didn't hate each other, we had just grown out of love. But, this course of action had knock on affects as we had taken on the shop as a couple and the split meant I was now out of a job and out of a place to live. Worse was to come.

Anj and I went through a few ups and downs. But she did know someone with a room to let in Ilford and both Kay and I lived there for a few weeks, even sleeping in the same bed but leading totally separate lives. Kay was often out with a guy who seemed to have become a sort of sex/live guru for her. While I visited Anj in her flat and later in the house her mother and new stepfather had purchased quite close to my old shop in Dagenham.

Kay found new employment and so did I in the form of another newsagents in Farr Avenue Barking, where |I worked for Martins. Eventually Kay moved away and I let the room in Ilford go because it seemed OK for me to stay in Anj's bedroom. How wrong I was!

Anj was adopted, as was her brother. In Anj's case it turned out her mother was part Indian and part European, while her father was Japanese. Apparently he was in Indian (where Anj was born) and had an affair then buggered off back to his wife and sons in Japan. As luck would have it Anj's mum worked for a Japanese bank where her boss had a thing for her. Bigger surprise was that he knew Anj's dad. And it even turned out that he had confessed all to his wife who was happy for him to bring a daughter in to the house (as they had several boys but no daughter). Her father was quite well off too and he was looking for her. But Anj didn't want to meet him, so the guy never realized how close he was to finding his long lost child.

Barry was apparently part English and part Indian, probably Seek. But no one came looking for him. Both of them had been brought up in Calcutta until they were about eleven or twelve. At this point their adopted mother left their adopted father and brought them back to England. It was a bit of a culture shock, to say the least.

While in India they had been in the lap of luxury. Dad was a top lawyer and mixed with the cream of society. He was Anj's mum's second husband, the first one being a Indian medical students who had run off with her best friend and a large amount of her money. And Anj's dad was also a huge Anglophile. Although pure Indian he spoke with a more clipped and posh British accent than most upper class Englishmen!

Anj and her brother were brought up in a large villa with several servants. And people of high social rank often visited, embassy staff, local diplomats, visiting doctors, lawyers and businessmen. They were taught the local culture, religion and language. At age ten Anj could talk two Indian languages, but she couldn't talk English. And it was only when they came to this country to stay that they learned English properly. Although when I met them they had no accent at all and their English was pretty much spot on.

So coming to London and living in a high rise and attending an English school was something of a come down for them. And going back to work for their mother was something of a culture shock too. But in the case of her mother she did keep true to form, meeting and eventually marrying someone from outside her own culture and ethnicity. In this case a very ugly and disagreeable Jamaican.

Up to the point they were married nothing was said about me staying. I didn't force myself on anyone and kept mainly to Anj's room. But as soon as they were married I was told I couldn't stay. Something of a problem as I had no where to go and no money to put down as a deposit on a flat anyway! And so started three months of me being homeless.

In just over a year I had gone from having a three bedroom house with a hundred foot garden, my own apple and pear trees, cats, etc. To, well, nothing! All I had was some clothes and my Volkswagen Passat, with a dented boot that didn't close properly where some twit had gone up my arse the day I bought it. And it was at the coldest time of the year.

I would wake up in the night, my back aching, freezing cold, rain banging down on the roof like tintacks and wonder who I had offended to end up like this? In the morning I would drag myself to the shop and wash and shave before anyone got there.

So passed a pleasant few months of me eating take away in my car and freezing to death in my sleeping bag. Anj visited me as often as she could, but her mother, who, disliked me intensely, did everything to split us up, even though we had become engaged.

The only thing that made life bearable was my new job and my assistant manager Mandy. Mandy was the exact opposite of Anj. Anj was short, dark, artistic, intelligent, shy and sexually backward. Mandy was tall, fair, earthy, sexy and outgoing, she was also engaged. However that did not stop us from having a long and passionate affair.

Mandy brightened my day by being there for me and because we could lock the office and have some fun too. But she would let me use the shower at her parents place, fetch me meals and wash my clothes for me too.

Eventually I found a bedsit near Barking Station. And with some help from my mum (again) I got a mortgage for it and moved in. It was meant to be temporary but I lived there with Anj for five years.

Anj and I also got married at Barking Registry office. Her brother was best man and Mandy was a bridesmaid, albeit a very unhappy one, she had asked me more than once to choose her over Anj and in later years I really wished I had. What's worse, is looking back on it now, I really can't see why I didn't!?

I left Martins and Mandy and moved on to work for Woolworths in Romford as a section manager. It was an education in several ways. I was in charge of more staff, it was far busier than anything I had known before and I had the biggest pratt on Earth as my General Manager and we hated each other.

I awoke one morning to go to work to find devastation

everywhere, trees down, roofs off, walls fallen over. It was 1987 and both Anj and I had managed to sleep through one of the biggest and most destructive storms the country had known!

Woolworths came and went as I was made redundant, having pissed the General Manager off once too often. However, he didn't get it all his own way, after 30 years with the company I helped put the final nail in his coffin and he was blocked from any chance of a promotion, several months later he left the company. I always warned people not to mess me with me, and he just didn't listen.

Within a short time I had found a new job with a company called Weider Health and Fitness. In this country only people in to bodybuilding or keep fit would have known them. But in the States they were well known and were responsible for the rise of people like Arnold Schwarzenegger who competed in their Mr Olympia contest. I was taken on as assistant manager and had a great time and saw a few stars too and not only of the bodybuilding field. Visitors to our store in Charring Cross included pop starts Limal and Marc Almond, boxer Barry McGuigan, athlete Collin Jackson, celeb Koo Stark, to name but a few. We also had Donna Hartley and Berry De Mey give seminars and got a visit from all time great Dorian Yates.

During all this I had moved my aikido class from the evening class to a private venue in Judd Street where Sensie Suzuki (a well known karate instructor taught). I still had a small but thriving class going on a Sunday, just after the hapkido class. However I had changed. Gone was the 11 stone wiry and lightening fast youth. Now, approaching my mid thirties I was in to weight training and I had blown up to over 14 stone (at one time at the height of my interest in bodybuilding I went 15 1/2 stone and had ideas of competing). These days I was slower but more powerful and more likely to take someone to the floor for a wrestle.

Eventually, despite some good times I left Weider to join Tandy. Back then a thriving British offshoot of the American electronics store. I joined as a trainee manager and worked my way through assistant manager to manger of my own store in Tottenham. And I made some good friends on the way.

It was while I was working in the Bishopsgate branch that I had a close encounter with a IRA bomb. While out for a drink one night with a couple of friends there was a loud bang (more a deep rumble) and the whole pub shook. Only about a quarter of a mile away a huge bomb had just ripped through the Natwest building and knocked out windows as far down as Liverpool Street, which is where we drinking. Within seconds we raced back to our shop, opposite the station, only to find everything already cordoned off. Funny that, as the police said they had no prior warning?

The place looked like the Blitz! Glass blown out everywhere, car alarms going off, smoke. And then a long trek as we were forced to leave the area by the police and walk to the next nearest station.

Too be honest my time as a manager in Tottenham was boring and the journey tiresome. Although we did have a laugh on match days. Everyone in the shop were Arsenal supporters, while we were on the main route to hated rivals Tottenham Hotspur. And oh we did laugh when the disgruntled fans wandered back passed us having lost at home. And being caring citizens we gave them a friendly wave and pissed our selves laughing. How we never got our windows put through is beyond me
At about this time I gave up on the ju jutsu. It was more because I just couldn't give it the time it required at the time, plus I never did get on as well with the Dagenham end of the club. But I had got my assistant instructors certificate by then and I had my certificate in kobudo.

By the time I was heading for black belt in ju jutsu Terry had moved the goalposts a little and it was a requirement not only to learn ju jutsu it's self but also to become proficient with several weapons, namely nunchuka, sai, stick, tonfa and katana. Terry had spent quite a lot of his own time and money (possibly not wisely) learning a kata in each weapon from Mike Finn. Mike, an ex police officer, was at the time the man with the most black belts in the world, something like 35 dans in about ten different disciplines. Only thing is, according to various sources he wasn't too good at any of them. But, that said, the forms were ok.

I spent more and more of my time in the gym trying to get bigger. I belonged to one of those spit and sawdust gyms were grunting was also a form of communication. And it was while I was doing an incredibly stupid weight on the incline leg press I decided to put my back out in a big way!

There I was with 600lbs on the bar, one rep, big breath, two, few stars, three, go for a fourth and...silly sod, don't lean forward as you press up and snap. Cut a long story short I was on my back for a week. Not funny when you need a pee and it takes you 20 minutes to crawl to the toilet.

I was however in the best place already, laying on the floor. The bedsit was so small we couldn't afford to have much furniture and so we slept on the floor. I did that for five years.

Around about now exit a couple of characters from my past. It's OK dont panic, they just left but didn't die. Number one Loch McPhee. Great guy and friend, but last time I saw him was when he came to fix a new door for me after I got burgled. Ummm, quick diversion burglars lowest of the low and bain of my life!

When I was about 15 the ex caretaker of our flats sold the master key on to some burglars, I walked in to find the place ransacked, not nice, worse when they may still have been there with knifes being carried around the house. When Kay and I broke up we stored some of our stuff (including my entire record collection) in our shop garage. Kids broke in and stole most of it.

So, two down and at that time I didn't know I had another three to go, but I did. Three times we got broken in to. First time someone took a sledgehammer to out double glazing, second they kicked the front door in and third time they took a chainsaw to it.

The little that we had disappeared quite quickly. It included the one and only thing I had from my dad, his service medal and a samurai dagger I had bought years earlier, that belonged to the Togukawa family (rulers of Japan).

Interesting little story here, on the second theft I was called by the police to say they had recovered some of my property. Turned out the detective involved was someone I knew and he managed to leave the evidence tags on with the accused name on it. Of course it was all an 'accident', but it did give me someone to look for, unfortunately for me I didn't find him, despite some effort.

Any way, as I was saying that was the last time I saw Loch. Dave Murphy was the next to go. Over the years I had bailed him out on a few occasions. But unbeknown to me he had borrowed money off of Anj and then failed to pay it back. It wasn't the fact he coerced money out of her, it was the fact he had gone behind my back to do it. I told him to sling his hook and never saw him again. We had been friends for over 20 years.

Like I said Anj and I spent five years in our dismal little bedsit. The only let off we had was when we visited her mum and brother. Her mum had moved to Peckham with her Jamaican husband. Barry had met a girl and spent much of his time at her place or in the company of her brother. And when we visited we would all go to a local pub for a few games of pool. My step father in law was a pratt and I tried to avoid him when ever I could.

An example of what a pillock this guy was can be drawn from a trip we made to Anj's aunt in Fleet. He drove us there and back. And on the return journey we got pulled over by the police, and ...get this....he got told to drive faster!

At about this time I made a startling discovery, as you grow older your hair falls out! Yes, I was going bald. It was one of those little revelations that indicate you are getting older after all.

At first I didn't take much notice as, in my case, it was just a matter of a higher hairline. But then I also noticed that I could see more or my head through the middle of my hair than round the sides. And so my first move towards emulating my hero Yul Brunner was put in place and I went for a number four crop. The number four didn't last long and I got myself some clippers and saved a fortune in hairdresser fees while giving myself a number one crop.

As our marriage moved on two things became evident, one was that Anj's ability in the bedroom was not going to improve, which was a pity as she was next to useless and also that the slim girl I married was rapidly being replaced by a somewhat overweight one! Further more she was addicted to one arm bandits! Very few nights went by that, on the way home from the bank she worked at, she didn't stop off to gamble her money in the arcades, or if I was with her a pub.

Her art started to take a backseat and she really didn't have much interest in anything, and certainly not me. But we still had the occasional interesting chat in the middle of the night   and played a few games of cards, so it wasn't a total loss, was it?

Sharing the bedsit with three cats wasn't so easy either. Especially when one of them decided to get the squirts one night. I can tell you now it is not a comfortable feeling laying there on the floor and in the dark and wondering what the nasty smell is. It gets worse when there is the sound of a very wet fart followed by a startled meow! And it hits rock bottom (pardon the pun) when this appears to be repeated all around the room as if there wasn't one cat at it, but about five or six! The clear up afterwards is even worse!!

Eventually we bought a three bedroom flat on the Gasgoigne Estate in Barking. Not the greatest place in the world but the flat was pretty big. And we didn't pay over the odds as we bought it off her cousin. I retained the bedsit with the idea of renting it out.

What should have been a great new start quickly declined in to a mediocre existence. We had a vast flat for just the two of us, I made one room my weights room and another a library with 1500 books in it. We got sky too and I spent hours watching and listening to the latest music especially the rock/grunge channels. We should have had the time of our life, but it just didn't happen.

To top it off my cat Blackie got ill and we had to have her put down. She was rarely a nice cat and was in fact more feral than domesticated, but I cried my eyes out when I left the vet. Yes I know big softie, but I always have been when it comes to animals.

Just when things had got as bad as they could I made an unexpected discovery. Mandy was working in Romford. And suddenly I found an excuse to pop and see her on my days off.

It wasn't long before our affair was back on, despite the fact she was married too. At least the bedroom saw some action, even if it was fairly brief and clandestine. But it wasn't meant to last and I found myself back in a rut again.

I left Tandy as the writing was on the wall. And not long after I went the company collapsed.

I moved in a totally new direction both geographically and product wise and joined Clinton Cards as a manager at their Surrey Keys branch. It paid the bills but was hardly riveting. But I did have nice staff and some helpful and friendly co managers. I stayed with them for about two and a half years.

Then I spotted a job with my old employer Martins. I had no idea it would change everything.

Chapter Ten - Third Time Lucky

The job wasn't overly exciting but certainly seemed a bit more interesting than spending day after day in a shop wishing the time would pass more quickly. And it did mean I got a company car. Although it also meant I had to pass a manual test (I had had an automatic licence for years). The job was working as a relief manager, standing in for shop managers while they were on holiday, off sick, etc and included a vehicle and meant working within the M25 area. Pay was OK and so were the prospects. I applied and was accepted almost immediately.

I said goodbye to Clintons and arrived at Martins HQ in Brentwood Essex one Monday morning 1995. I turned up and got shown to a waiting area where, like all new employees, I sat a little nervously wondering what the day would hold. What I didn't expect was that it would hold my next wife!

A guy turned up, another relief manager like myself. And then two women arrived. One of them was quite tall and slim, with long fair hair. She wore glasses so might not have attracted all men, but she had a great pair of legs and figure and a winning smile and her name turned out to be Trish.

The training was partly done local to London and part

done in Wolverhampton. And the first week saw me paired with another guy in North London. But I much preferred the training in Wolves as it gave me a chance to steal glances at Trish as we sat in the classroom.

I couldn't believe my luck when Trish and I were paired up to be trained in a shop in Corringham for two weeks. We got on like a house on fire too! Although it transpired she was living with a guy she had left her husband for. So my prospects of anything happening seemed some what remote.

Anyway, the course moved back to Wolves and also towards it's end. On our last night we all got suitably pissed and played pool. And Trish and I seemed to spend a fair part of the evening together.

And when it came time to hit the sack Trish, another guy and myself just couldn't quite switch off and spent the reminder of the evening playing cards in my room.

Trish fell asleep on my bed and after a bit of a discussion it was decided to leave her there. The other guy went back to his room and I snuggled down next to Trish to sleep. Later I awoke as did Trish and one thing lead to another....Well I wont paint a picture. Although a little later it turned out that Trish had never been to sleep at all and it was all part of the plan.

We travelled back from Wolverhampton together the next day. Holding hands most of the way. Trish had parked her car outside my flat in Barking and it was with a real sinking feeling that I watched her drive away, even though we had arranged to meet the next day in Romford.

The next few days were some of the most up and down ones I can remember having. Within a short time I confessed what had happened to Ang, who, initially, did not take it well. But within a few days we had sorted out that I would be leaving. Fortunately I still had the little bed sit but for the first few days I just slept in one of the spare rooms.

I met Trish in Romford as arranged and it quickly transpired that both of us wanted out of our relationships and she told me she was moving out of her boyfriends and back to her mum's. It would have been nice to report on a fairytale romance from this point, but you know what life is like and this was no different!

Firstly her now ex boyfriend turned out to be a pain in the arse. He tried stirring things up more than once. And he made the mistake of threatening me as well, although he did only ever do that from the other end of a phone line and never in person. Secondly I was not flavour of the month with Trish's mum, an iceberg that was very slow to melt as it turned out.

Having passed our training Trish was posted to a branch in Oxford, while I took over one in Cricklewood or little Ireland as it should be called. As part of her conditions of service Trish was able to rent a company paid for room in a house on the edge of Sommertown and, I unofficially moved in with her. And while she did a short trip to work everyday I commuted down the M40 and A40 to West London. And although not ideal it did allow for a few nice evenings out at the local pubs and a chance to get to know each other better.

It came as something of a shock to find that in the not too distant future I would become a father for the first time, when Trish revealed she was pregnant very early on in our relationship! But it also meant that we needed to secure somewhere a bit more permanent than the dingy bed sit I still had or the rented room Trish had. So we approached our employer, who, as luck would have it, owned more than a few premises it was willing to rent out. And before long we moved in to our first proper home together above a Martin's at Martins Corner Dagenham.

Joshua John Lancaster arrived bright and early one morning in October 1995, and, as any parent will tell you, life was never quiet the same again! And it wasn't long before Trish and I were strolling arm in arm behind a pram.

It also wasn't long before Josh was sitting there watching me teach aikido. I still had a few faithful follower's at this point although the class had shrunk and many of my older pupils had fallen by the wayside.

Many people probably think of martial arts clubs as a place you just do fighting. But many take on a much more familiar feel with people becoming good friends and staying so over many years. Some of my pupils had trained with me for more than ten years.

But I had to admit the one class a week was more than

enough at that stage. It was a grind travelling to the centre of London every week even by car, when the traffic was at it's lightest. And although I often had Trish and Josh for company this wasn't always the case and it could be boring making it back alone. And to be honest I felt stale and in need of a new challenge.

The new challenge arrived in more ways than one! In 1996 I started a new job with Total oil as a manager, but it was not that that provided the challenge or the surprise. Trish had been having 'woman's problems' for a while and we went to the doctor and later the hospital. I was with Trish when she came out from some tests with a sheepish look on her face to be told one of the problems was due to her being pregnant again.

Another challenge arrived by way of our former employer Martin's who wanted us out of their flat ASAP, I don't think me taking them to an industrial tribunal and giving them a bloody nose helped. But we had to move in to a little one bedroom affair in Dagenham in a road called White Barn Lane. And it was here that Luke Adam Lancaster arrived very suddenly one evening in June 1997. He was even quicker than Josh who had arrived in just an hour and half , but Luke took about half that time and took both Trish, myself and the midwife by surprise.

However with two boys to look after and accommodate we needed to get out of the small flat we had and we managed this by getting a shared ownership property in Baden Powell Close Dagenham. This allowed us the opportunity to get a pet rabbit as well as we had a huge garden, and later still our first dog a rescue Staffordshire

Bull Terrier called Cassie. And Trish was soon back out to work too and things were going ok. But the big challenge still had not arrived yet.

It did arrive later that year in the form of a small Chinese gentleman called Lu Jun Hai. Trish was at that time working for a flooring company and had got friendly with a customer called Ed. Trish obviously discussed me and the boys and when Ed heard I was in to martial arts suggested that Trish bring me down to the Havering Town show where he was going to be involved in a kung fu demonstration. He was at pains to stress he and the other members of the team were quite new to it and had only been training for a couple of months, but the instructor was a Chinese master with bags of experience.

So one nice August day we had a wander down to the show in Hornchurch and watched the demonstration. It was pretty basic, but when the Chinese master showed off some moves I was more than impressed, little did I know he was already in his late fifties at that point.

The master or Sifu was Lu Jun Hai a 6th generation practioner of Shaolin Mizong kung fu. I later discovered he was a Grand master in not only kung fu but also a rare Chinese sword form as well as Tai Chi. I didn't know it then but I had stumbled across a true treasure!

I started training under Sifu Lu a few weeks later and within only a couple of months was hooked. But not only that I also realised this was the challenge I had been looking for. I had little idea of how much it would change me then, but one thing was plain enough, my time with aikido was over.

Eric and Graham, two of my black belts were handed the keys to the kingdom and told to run the club for themselves. It was my intention to pop down and oversee things from a distance for a while but within a few weeks my focus had shifted to kung fu only and I left them to their own devices. For me it was an end of an era, but new adventures awaited.

Chapter 11 - Lost Track Boxing

I was used to hard work and pain in the martial arts but it had been a while since I had trained under someone else, and the movement and technique involved different muscle groups. For months I felt too stiff and awkward for kung fu and honestly doubted how far I could get.

The pain was different too, I was used to my arms being twisted or a sudden palm heel to my chin. But kung fu introduced 'knocking arms', a very painful method of hardening the arms and legs by slamming them against someone else's limbs. I was bruised almost the entire time. And the new wider stances and exercises to stretch the legs and make them supple were almost as bad.

Back then we had classes of up to and over thirty students and you could sometimes be kept in a pose for minutes at a time while Sifu walked around and made sure everyone was standing correctly. Often my legs were shaking by the time he let us move. He was also happy to demonstrate technique and explain practical applications but often at the expense of a split lip...us not him!

Sifu Lu had arrived in London direct from Shanghai, China and spoke virtually no English. Therefore the admin for the class as well as the translation from

Chinese to English and vice versa was done by a Chinese guy called Han.

Han seemed a pretty good guy and acted as Sifu's second. He also put a lot of effort in to arranging demonstrations, setting up classes and keeping sure everything ran ok. He had three young boys who also swelled the classes numbers.

We learned from Sifu (via Han) that what we were doing was called Lost Track Boxing and was several hundred years old and could be traced back to the famous Shaolin temple in China. Shaolin was the spiritual home of kung fu as well as the birth place of Chan (Zen) buddhism. These days a lot of people are aware of the various shows and demo's done by the Shaolin Monks, but back then it was not so well known and most people's knowledge of kung fu was from watching David Carradine in the show of the same name or seeing Bruce Lee films.

It came out over the weeks and months, and eventually years, that our particular style of kung fu could be traced back to 1722. And that it had been handed down from master to disciple for six generations. The style contains elements of other martial arts too, namely Xing-I, Tai Chi and Bagua. But on top of this Sifu also knew numerous types of weapons and how to use them.

Mizong is a well respected though little known style and like many martial art's it's origins are steeped in a haze of fact, half truth's and myths. And most people (or at least martial art's film buffs) are totally unaware they have seen the style portrayed on film by Bruce Lee in 'Fist of Fury' and again by Jet Li in 'Fearless'.

Sun Tong was the first master of Mizong and was an exponent of several styles and practices including joint locking and pressure point strikes. He spent ten years in the Shaolin monastery before travelling around China teaching and practising his art. He passed what he knew on to several students, one of whom was Chen Shan the second master of Mizong. The name it's self can be translated in several ways, but the most popular interpretations are Secret Buddhist Sect Boxing and Lost Track Boxing.

One of the greatest and best known exponents of Mizong was Hou Yuanjia (1869-1909) who used the style to become one of the best fighters of his time. And it is he who is played by Jet Li in 'Fearless'.

The fifth generation heir and master to the system was Lu Zhendou. He worked as a Chinese medical practioner as well as a bodyguard. One of his clients was a warlord Chang Hsueh Liang, who was infamous for kidnapping Chang Kai Shek, the then leader of China.

Lu Zhendou was an exceptional martial artist and became all Chinese Champion, back in the days when to do so meant displaying an open hand form, a weapon form and then fighting the other competitors. And it was not unusual for people to be injured or even killed during these competitions. Lu Zhendou passed on his expertise to his children, one of whom would become the sixth generation master of Mizong and that was Lu Jun Hai, my sifu.

Sifu Lu Jun Hai was a marvel, not only was he fast and flexible for his age he was also considered a 'national treasure' by the Chinese government for his in-depth knowledge of Chinese martial arts. He had started kung fu under his father aged six and went on to become the captain of the Shanghai martial arts youth team. Later he held several high ranking positions within the Shanghai martial arts community and also was technical director on TV shows involving kung fu. And he was a level one international judge with the Jingwu Martial Arts Academy, the same academy founded by Hou Yuanjia.

Pretty soon I was practicing kung fu when ever I could although another change of job did interfere with my training sometimes. I had started work with a duty free retailer working out of London City Airport and now worked shifts.

The new job meant I worked 12 hour shift's three days on and three days off. The journey was not bad and the money OK, but it did upset the rhythm of my training. But I had a garden big enough to cope with me jumping around in it on my day's off and keeping up some training even when I could not get to class.

Over the next three years we trained hard and gained several members who would stay with the club and Sifu Lu for the duration. These included Gary Matthews, Adam Lynch and Kevin Kilnminster. And during those years I would become firm friends with my training partner Ed Hutton.

There were other characters who came in at this point to play cameo roles and some who left and not always on good terms. One of these was the very man who had helped set Sifu Lu up with employment and classes in this country, Han.

We had heard of a guy called Robert Simpson through Han and knew that the guy was partly responsible for bringing Sifu here from China and that he ran his own classes near or in Luton, apart from that we knew little about him. So it came as a surprise one night that some of Sifu Lu's students from London arrived with Robert to announce that Sifu was being 'used' by Han. Unbeknown to us Han had being running our instructor ragged getting him to teach Han and his own children anytime and anywhere he wanted. Unfortunately due to his lack of English Sifu had been unable to tell anyone what was going on until he confided in a Chinese student at the central London class he ran. They in turn had contacted Robert who took it upon himself to speak to the Essex contingent of Sifu's pupils.

Not only was Sifu being kept on a very short leash but his living conditions were very poor (with he and his wife living in a cramped room) and his wages were almost non existent. Thus were the mighty fallen, Han who we had relied on to organise event's and demo's and help run the class and interrupt for Sifu had been using him for his own benefit, but not any more.

I only spoke to Han once after that and that was to tell him (over the phone) not to come near Sifu, me or anyone else at the class. To say tempers were running a bit high was an understatement.

But, good often comes out of bad and within weeks we could see the improvement in Sifu's demeanour. And it was at this time that he started to rely more on certain members of the class. He also took the opportunity to name the club Zhenwei Academy.

By 2000 myself and Ed were among a number of people who had attained black belts in Mizong. And not far behind us were people like Andy Hall, Kevin and 'Ryan' Lam. But in 2002 after nearly five year's training Sifu decided he wanted us to enter our first competition in of all places Baltimore USA!

We flew out to the US with Robert Simpson and his sister Suzie, both of whom were international referee's and well known to the American's, not least for the fact than their Sifu Grandmaster Huang Chien Liang was a major player in American kung fu and the All American Championship we were attending. We had a two week stay ahead of us with a lot of training (twice daily) and even marching practice for the grand entrance to the event as the UK team.

I could easily write a whole book about that one trip but let us just say there was training, eating, drinking, more drinking and a pretty good time had by all. Well nearly all, we did have a few mishaps along the way including me nearly missing the competition altogether when I hit myself in the leg with a 'dadao' (or large Chinese halberd).

Overall the competition went well and afforded us the

chance to see other exponents of kung fu and other styles.
It also reacquainted us with Hon Lee one of Sifu's pupils
who had trained with him in China.

We had first met Hon when he came to the UK to take
his discipleship. Kung fu can, in some schools, still be
very traditional. And people are not allowed to just
wander off and teach who and what they want, that is if
they are allowed to teach at all. And in Mizong under
Sifu Lu this was very much the case.

Back in China Sifu had 29 disciples, people who he
thought of as worthy to continue the teaching and
tradition of the style. Hon had become number 30 and the
first non Chinese disciple, for though he was of Chinese
blood Hon was an American and had served in the
Marines as a Lieutenant Colonel in Vietnam. Although
we did not know it at the time it would later transpire he
had worked for the CIA as well.

Over the following years we were, as both individuals
and a club, to meet Hon and his co-instructor Reza
Momenan and their students on a number of occasions.
And for many of us who do not have family in the States
this became the next best thing as they are a great bunch
of people.

The competition we entered for was the forms
competition. Sifu was of the opinion that sparring was
not a good idea for two reasons, firstly too dangerous (he
himself had badly injured someone during sparring) and
secondly sparring doesnt allow us to express Mizong as it
should be (gloves and too many rules). So we opted for
forms (what they call kata in Karate), prearranged

routines for individuals and pairs including empty hand and weapons. Some of the forms are hundreds of years old and were practised by people who used the art in a lot more violent way than now.

Ed and I were favourites from our team to get a medal in the two man form. Of course, how many times do favourites not win. When it came to it I messed up the very first move and that was us out of it straight away. Andy and Ryan ended up taking gold and Ed and I were devastated.

Fortunately we were both in other events and more importantly (especially for me) was that they were awarding bronze for both third **and** fourth places. Ed went on to get a bronze in another event and so did I but only by virtue of finishing fourth.

But that said it was a huge competition with about 700 people competing. The whole thing had been quite an eye opener, not a brilliant start but ok. And we arrived home to some very happy family members and a little bit of local fame. And I tried my hand at writing and got an article about our trip printed in 'Combat' magazine.

Chapter 12 - Adding to the Family Tree while Flashing the Blue Lamp

In 2003 I left the Airport and took up employment with the Metropolitan Police as a Police Community Support Officer (PCSO). It was a new role and afforded me the opportunity to join a uniformed service like so many of my ancestors. Of course it also meant more shift work.

One good thing about the job (apart from the pay) was getting to do more combat training (even if most of it was crap and just an arse covering exercise) and getting to use the skills I already had for real. And it didn't take long I knocked a guy out within the first month of being on the streets when he attacked some fellow officers.

I was also directly involved in major events like the aftermath of the 2005 London bombings. And I lost count of the amount of cordons I stood on, everything from cannabis factories to armed robberies and murder.

2003 was the year of only our third competition (we had visited Liverpool for one prior to this but the judging was awful and I was very disappointed not to place at all). The competition was in Luton and run by Robert Simpson and was the British Open event and included competitors from around the world. Zhen Wei did well and I won a first place and two second place medals.

In 2004 things really took off! March saw the club competing at the Southern Area Championships in Maidstone, Kent, run by the British Council for Chinese Martial Arts (BCCMA) and I came away with a silver and two bronze medals. Later in the year we competed in Milton Keynes at the National Championships for the BCCMA and I won medals in four events including two silver's and two bronze's. And this set us up nicely for the big event of the year and our biggest challenge so far The first European Kuoshu Cup in Neu-Ulm Germany.

We arrived in Germany on the Thursday competed for two days over the weekend and then flew home, after some sight seeing on the Monday. But obviously it was the Saturday and Sunday that was important to me and to the club, although maybe even more so for me as the team Captain.

The opening ceremony was (like the American Open) very upbeat with speeches and all the teams lined up by country. With ninety-five percent of the UK team being from the Zhen Wei Academy.

There was a really touching moment when Sifu Lu was given a birthday cake by Grandmaster Huang. And he was obviously touched by the whole affair and the attention.

The competition was another well attended affair and the home team was massive and expecting to do very well. But I don't think they were expecting the onslaught from the British contingent that was about to wash over them!

I did my own humble little bit by taking two first places, a second and a third. I kicked off by winning the senior men's weapon section using the daedo and then topped that off by winning the two man open hand form section with Ed against really stiff competition! And we were not so far from adding a second gold against a very large field in the two man weapons section (where we did a broad sword V spear form), eventually placing second. Finally I won a bronze with my display of Xing-i.

If you look at my photo taken with Ed (in the photo section) you can see how emotional I was. I can identify when I see sportsman, especially athletes, boxers and other martial artist's, celebrating a big win and on the verge of tears. It is a combination of years of training and putting in hour upon hour of effort, working through injuries, up's and down's trying to balance it with the rest of your life, work and family. Combined with that nagging doubt that you will never achieve what you think you are capable of and that all the time the clock is running down. And for me that last point was very important as I had just become European Champion at the ripe old age of 48!

To say the German's were shell shocked was an understatement and was summed up by Alex, the event's organiser's, comment on the presentation of my last cup when he said something along the line of 'if I see you collecting one more cup there is going to be trouble', albeit said in good humour. The results not only saw many individual successes but also the overall team cup coming our way, much to the delight of team coach Sifu Lu!

Although the winning of the various competitions was great fun and (all joking apart) becoming European champion was really humbling, an event that took place earlier in the year over shadowed
these achievements. That event was being added to the family tree of Mizong kung fu when I and several other senior students were granted the privilege of becoming official disciples of Sifu Lu.

On 24th January 2004 Ed Hutton, Gary Matthew, Kevin Kilnminster, Wen Ting, Xun Dong, Spencer Attridge and myself became the first British disciples of Sifu Lu and 7th generation heirs to the system.
This took place in the house Sifu and his wife shared in Gidea Park and involved us having to write a letter stating why we thought we were good enough to become disciples. On the day we each handed Sifu the letter and a red envelope containing money. Sifu then lighted some incense sticks and called on the Mizong ancestors so that we could each be introduced to them. Each of us then kowtowed in front of the little makeshift alter he had erected, which, along with the incense sticks housed a picture of Sifu's father.

One by one we greeted our 'family' ancestors and became part of a family tree that was just a little under 300 years old. But the importance of this day was more than just a ceremony, it also moved the burden of continuing the art of Mizong from Sifu's shoulders to ours. Now upon his retirement or death we would become the next generation of masters with the sole right to teach the system in it's entirety!

Over the next few years the bond between the disciples and Sifu Lu became stronger and stronger. As with all such Chinese institutions we considered him our father and the other disciples as brothers and sisters. If someone was in trouble we gathered around to help. And when ever possible we got together for a drink and something to eat, most often at Sifu's with he and his wife cooking for us and providing a few beers, before sitting down to plan our next competition or how the club would run or just to hear some stories from Sifu.

I also progressed from patrolling the streets in Ilford to training new recruits at the central Metropolitan Police College in Hendon. My time in Ilford as a PCSO was an eventful one and set me up with a few good war stories for when I was teaching. And I will always be grateful to Sergeant Grahame Clarke who guided me through my tour of duty and who recommended me for promotion to trainer.

Just a little aside for some of the people who were not keen on the idea of PCSO's. During our first year in Ilford Town centre crime reduced by 30%, there were no changes other than we were walking the beat where no one had before. And we were much more hands on than many people believed and that was without all the safety equipment the police had. In fact with some of us the police would happily stand back and let us get someone pinned down before stepping in.

OK I know, plenty of stories about crap PCSO's or ones who had no idea, and we had both on our team too. Two got them selves the sack and another got nicked as well. But the others were pretty good and made a lot of difference to the local community. Moreover as a trainer I saw a lot of PCSO's go on to make the grade and pass out as police officers too.

I also didn't spend my entire time locked away as a trainer. I now had the opportunity to become a special constable and after my classroom input went back to Grahame in Ilford to complete my probation as a police officer.

I was now allowed to go out on patrol and 'nick' people a couple of times a month and get paid for it. But I joined the Arts and Antiques Unit at Scotland Yard under then head of the unit Sergeant Vernon Rapley. And had fun getting involved in art fraud cases and art theft. My first arrest for them was of a guy for a £15 million fraud.

Later I gained the rank of sergeant and was involved in some of the bigger events in London like the TUC march, Olympics and the riots. I also got to continue with my police self defence training too (whopee)

Anyway, enough of that and back to kung fu. Between 2005 and 2007 I picked up 15 medals at the National Championships, including winning and retaining the two man empty hand forms title and the two man weapons forms title at advanced level every year with my partner Ed Hutton. Not a bad achievement even if I do say so myself.

I mentioned before that excelling in the martial arts come with an injury cost. But this is even higher when you are training for competition with a partner. Over the years Ed and I have done more than our fair share of damage to each, mainly because we don't pull our punches or our kicks. But it was that attitude that won us so many titles.

Some of the injuries I can recall are, for instance, when Ed elbowed me and broke my ribs, when he slapped me across the collar bone and I collapsed and the numerous times he has smacked me in the face. On the reverse I have broken his fingers several times, split his lip and dislocated his finger.

Some of the injuries during competition were quite good too, like the time he cut my leg open with a sword and the time he nearly cut my spear in half and left me with a large cut down the middle of my head. But like I said we don't pull punches, just never think because something is a prearranged routine it is not dangerous!

Chapter 13 - 'Top of the World Ma'

2008 was an interesting year. That year we did some demo's at the Senie Show, for those not in the know a very big yearly affair that takes place at venues like EXCEL and attract thousands of martial artist's and non martial artist's. A video of us is still on Youtube.

But it was also the year we went back to the States. This time we stayed in Virginia and visited Hon Lee and Reza's club several times as well as being taken out by them and their students on various day trips. We then all attended the US open in Baltimore. And guess what!? I did it again fourth place, OK but I did place third in another event too.

Unfortunately Ed could not make the trip so I was left to my own devices when it came to the competition. Still I did come away with a medal and so did the other guys.

Competition wise we now had a bit of a lull and just did not train for anything for two years. Just as well really as during this time my health went down the pan in more ways than one.

While at work one day I felt a little off. This turned in to a big off and I more or less collapsed. I managed to convince my sergeant that I could drive home, but by the time I got there I was almost out at the wheel. Trish rushed me to a medical centre and they in turn called an ambulance when they found my blood sugar had dropped off to just 2.1 milligrams (apparently most people would have been in a coma by then).

Extensive tests followed over the next few years and varying conditions considered and then ruled out. They thought I may have diabetes, then pancreatic cancer and several other things. To this day they still have no idea what is wrong, but it did knock me back a bit, as did the spin offs from the tests and other conditions that also arose at the same time.

It transpired that I had a mild ectopic heart beat, or in other words my heart skipped the occasional beat (funny because in most other ways it was more than fine and I had a heart beat that stayed as lower as fifty beats or so a minute). And I was suffering from an inherited cholesterol condition which saw my bad cholesterol count at 11 (the safe range being under five), the doctor immediately put me on tablets and told me the happy news that I would be on them for the rest of my life.

On top of all this I was getting a bad pain in my left knee so, again after tests, it turned out I had arthritis in both knees and hips probably caused by aikido and ju jutsu. Later tests would also show I had it in one of my elbows as well, which did explain why I could no longer straighten it fully. Many of the problems were due to injuries and all the tests and x-rays revealed that I had several undiagnosed fractures, which had healed without me even knowing the bone was broken. They included a break to my ankle, two in my arm and one in my hand.

OK so here it comes. Even after all those years training and meditating etc etc, it still hit me for six. And I still needed to talk to a councillor. See even big brave martial artist's can crack.

I should mention that since our discipleship ceremony we had had several in's and out's. Out went Spencer, always odd and just got odder to the point where he grew a long beard and buggered off never to be seen again. Dong also seemed to loose interest and faded in to the background and Wen Ting went off to work in the Far East, which, was a shame. And although not a disciple the departure of Andy Hall for Australia was a big blow for many of us, especially Ed and myself who were quite close to him.

In came Adam Lynch who Sifu also accepted as a disciple as did Andy Lee another disciple. And a little later Sifu would also take on Andy Denney and his wife Shu and lastly Errol Armstrong.

Should also probably mention at this point that my sons Joshua and Luke had also taken up Mizong as well. In Joshua's case with some reluctance but Luke had taken to it like a duck to water. Both reached black belt but in Luke's case he also entered and medalled at several competitions including winning the National Championship for his age group.

Anyway I got back to training, albeit a little subdued and a bit more careful than before. Then in 2010 Sifu decided he was taking us to China for the 10th Grand Wu

Shu World Fair in Shanghai. This is basically the World Championships for Wu Shu. Again for those not in the know Wu Shu is a modern derivative of kung fu. It is much more flowery and far less practical but does involve some exciting and sometimes very athletic routines. And the championship also had a traditional kung fu element and it was that part of the competition we were interested in.

Prior to going out to China I was invited to talk on BBC Essex by Xante Bearman. It was a good chance to talk about kung fu and get our name out there and I was on air for about 15 minutes.

The trip to Shanghai was not all about the competition. It was also a trip home to see family for Sifu and Simu and a chance for us to see the sights and also meet some of Sifu's old students.

The competition came right at the beginning of our two week stay in China. And once again I think we surprised a few people! Once again Ed was unable to make the trip but I entered two competitions in the senior division and came away with a World Championship gold medal for a form with the daedo and a silver medal for my demonstration of Xing-i. Luke also won two silver medals in his age group. The other guys did just as well winning individual and team medals in several categories and we were unofficially voted the best team by the judges. BUT, we are talking China here so there had to be a down and that was we were not allowed to pick up our medals at the event. While everyone else (who was Chinese) got to stand there and be awarded their medals, we got ours from Sifu who in turn had been handed them by the judges. It was a shame because it was one of the few down points of the trip.

One thing that did come across was the high esteem Sifu was held in by his peers. And this was reinforced when we went to the park for a training session with his old pupils.

We arrived to a big banner welcoming the brothers and sisters (that's us) from the UK. We were expecting just to join in the training but it ended up with everyone doing demonstrations and half the park watching us. But it was great knowing that this is where Sifu and his father had both trained. And it was important enough for the Chinese Government to declare the area a national heritage site with it's own plaque.

The rest of the trip was mainly taken up with site seeing including visits to a Buddhist temple and various museums and heritage sites. There was a fair amount of drinking and eating, although Chinese food in China bares little resemblance to Chinese food in the UK, a fact that was pointed out by my wife Trisha and my eldest Joshua several times.

We returned to the UK with the knowledge that we had done just about everything that could be done for Sifu and for the Zhen Wei Academy and the UK. But like so many activities not many people ever found out. So we were to a great extent unsung heroes.

Chapter 14 - In conclusion

Life since the World Championship has gone on and for the most part we all continue to train as hard and when we can. Since then I have added Tai chi to my repertoire, have left the police and taken up business in several new areas, including writing and running my own freelance first aid concern.

The other guys all still train, but like me one or two are suffering now. And despite being 73 Sifu is still teaching, although Kevin has now taken over running the Tai chi, Kevin and Adam will be taking on running some of the clubs when Sifu retires, Gary has started his own clubs as had Andy Denney. And I sit in the background happy to give advice as the senior brother in the UK.

I also managed to get myself about a bit. If you check out the national police site for officer training you will see me getting handcuffed for the sake of handcuff training (lost the feeling in my thumb for three months due to that). And I and the others have turned up in a few papers etc.

I hope along the way I have not upset too many people with my revelations that most martial artist's, even very good ones, like a drink. And that sometimes we can be pretty petty and stupid. And becoming a top notch martial artist doesn't always mean you don't remain a complete plank too!

There is still a lot of bigotry in the martial arts world as well as a lot of people trying to reinvent the wheel when there was nothing wrong with it in the first place. And it still amazes me that people are stupid enough to think that one martial art or combat system is any better than another. Or that people can come up with mind bogglingly stupid phrases like ' This is real combat not martial arts'. What they normally mean is this is a thug teaching self defence and leaving out all the safety checks, like respect for all life, that most martial arts apply.

There is no ultimate martial art, Bruce Lee was not the second coming and there is no easy route to becoming a good fighter or martial artist, and remember, the two do not even always go together! And don't forget MMA (mixed martial arts) is a sport, it has rules just like boxing and anything with rules is limited.

There are plenty of classes around these days, have a look around and you may be lucky, like me, to come across something you enjoy. It can be a great way to make new friends and keep fit, you just have to find the right club and teacher for you.

Bruce Lee was right about one thing, you take what suits you and make it work for you. Everyone is different, height, weight, reach, strength, speed and how you think. Find a martial art or system that works for you. Work hard and don't expect miracles. And don't make it up as you go along, someone else has already done that and probably done a better job too.

Lastly I hope this may give some people the will to go on and try things they have not done before, or return to something they once tried. Remember your never too old or too disabled to try.

Good luck!

Glossary of Terms

Aikido - Japanese martial art meaning 'way of the harmonious spirit'

Aiki-jutsu - martial sub system derived from Ju-jutsu

Bagua - Chinese internal fighting system

bodo/bo-jutsu - Japanese fighting system using a stick

Bokken - Wooden practice sword
Boxing - Western fighting art now a sport

Budo - Japanese code of ethics for the samurai

Bujutsu - Samurai weaponry

Chan/Zen - Buddhist sect

Chin-a - Locking and throwing using the joints

Chi/Ki - Energy that martial artists use to perform certain feats

Chin Ping (or Qing Ping) - Chinese ancient sword fighting system

Dadoe - Chinese weapon something like a European halberd

Dan/duan - black belt grades (normally starting at one and progressing up to ten or in some cases higher)

Goshin Jutsu - style of Ju-jutsu

Hakama - Divided skirt worn by the samurai and some martial artists

Hapkido - Korean martial art

Iaido - Japanese art of drawing and cutting using a katana (Samurai sword)

I-ching - Book of Changes

Jodo - Japanese art of stick fighting

Judo - Competition sport derived from Ju-jutsu ' gentle or compliant way'

Ju-jutsu - Japanese fighting system used by the samurai

Jukka Ryu - Style of Ju-jutsu

Karate - Okinawan fighting system ' way of the empty hand'

Kata - series of pre planned moves involving one or more people

Katana - Samurai sword

Kobudo - Mastery of some of the Japanese weapons

Kung fu - General term covering several hundred different Chinese styles of fighting

Kyudo - Japanese archery

Mizong - Style of kung fu 'lost track boxing'

Mochzoe - Form of meditation

Ninja/Ninjutsu - Person who does ninjutsu/ art of stealth incorporating a fighting style used by spies/assassins in Japan

Nunchuka - Rice flails used as a weapon

Preying Mantis - Style of kung fu

Sai - farming implement adapted for fighting, looks like a big fork with a long central tine

Shaolin - A Buddhist temple in China birth place of Chan Buddhism and centre of excellence for kung fu, also a style of kung fu

Shodakan - Sub style of aikido

Sifu (Chinese)/Sensie (Japanese) - Instructor or teacher

Simu (Chinese) - Mother Teacher

Tai Chi - Style of kung fu using slow movements and

considered beneficial for health

Tae Kwon Do - Korean art similar to karate ' way of the hand and foot'

Taoism - Chinese religious / philosophical system

Tomiki - Kenji Tomiki founder of Tomiki style aikido

Tonfa - farming implement used for fighting, long wooden block with a handle on one side

Xing-i - Internal style of kung fu

Yoga - Indian system of movements for health and meditation

Yoshinkan - Style of aikido

Other books by Karl Lancaster

Sex Stories for a Mature Woman - six erotic short stories following the exploits of mature women taking on a new adventure.

The Trials of Jules Jovian - Eight stories following the sexual exploits of a woman from her teens to her fifties

Coming soon by Karl Lancaster

Encyclopedia of the Martial Arts - a look at the various martial arts still in use today.

Printed in Great Britain
by Amazon

27536427R00096